We Are Experiencing a Slight Delay

ALSO BY GARY JANETTI

Do You Mind If I Cancel?

Start Without Me

We Are Experiencing a Slight Delay

(tips, tales, travels)

Gary Janetti

HARPER

An Imprint of HarperCollins*Publishers*

HarperCollins books may be purchased for educational, business,
or sales promotional use. For information, please email the Special
Markets Department at SPsales@harpercollins.com.

FIRST EDITION

Designed by Bonni Leon-Berman

Library of Congress Cataloging-in-Publication Data has been applied
for.

ISBN 978-0-06-332974-4

24 25 26 27 28 LBC 5 4 3 2 1

For Brad
and for everyone else I've met while traveling
(but mostly Brad)

Contents

We Are Experiencing a Slight Delay

chapter one

Wellness

I'm not by nature a wellness person. It's not that I have anything against being well; what sane person would? It's more about the type of person that wellness attracts. The kind of person who holds eye contact so long, you are, inevitably, forced to look away first. My eyes tend to dart around, stopping at the other person's eyes only occasionally to check in, not trying to sear into their soul over a conversation about how many glasses of water to drink a day.

Besides, no wellness specialist I have ever come across has particularly seemed all that well to me to begin with. It's more like they are projecting the idea of wellness, while just underneath, they are (like all of us) ready to snap.

I can usually get even the most serene person to have a bit of edge creep into their voice within five minutes. It's a game I like to play with myself. It's like non-wellness is my wellness. Only once I see that you are also fucked-up, will I ever start to relax. I don't care about your thoughts on the amount of antioxidants in broccoli, but I do care if someone having a cell phone conversation next to you on an airplane makes you want to jam a pen into their throat.

I don't know why I'm always looking for a crack, a flaw, a blemish. Something where I can finally say, "Ah, *there* you are! *That's* who this person is!"

I much more relate to a person who talks about being lazy, than one who talks about being busy. Who cares if you're busy? And busy doing WHAT? I'm assuming everyone is going around doing stuff, you don't need to tell me. I'm not going to give you anything for being the most busy person I know. I'll never care. But if you tell me all you did yesterday was sit on the couch and watch TV, I'm riveted.

The self-congratulatory-ness of the wellness community seems to attract these same "very busy" people I'm always trying to avoid. They all go on wellness retreats in order to talk about how they're there to *not* talk about how busy they are. And, let's be honest, how busy can you really be if you're able to stop your life for a week to go on a wellness retreat? Not very.

Telling someone you're busy is like telling someone you're funny. If you have to say it, we know it's not true. A bride doesn't go around on her wedding day telling everyone how beautiful she is—which makes it that much easier to tell her she's gorgeous, no matter what she looks like. (Whoever said all brides are beautiful was an ugly bride.)

I can think of nothing worse than a wellness retreat. To me, a vacation is doing exactly what I would do at home, only with better weather and room service. I don't want a list of activities designed to push me beyond any mental or physical limits I may have. I *like* my mental and physical limits where they are. That's why I put them there. I don't need to go to, say, Scottsdale, Arizona, to prove to myself that I can climb farther up a rock wall than a mother of three from Connecticut. And I don't need to eat gluten-free meals with a group of strangers dressed in ill-fitting spandex. The only people I want to see in workout clothes are Olympians and college athletes. Definitely not dissatisfied middle-aged lumps who can afford to piss away money on wellness.

I grew up in a middle-class home in Queens in the '70s and '80s. Wellness was what you were when you weren't sick. It was the baseline. Most of the time that's what you were. Now it is something we aspire to, like the peak of Everest. (A place where the very rich pay a fortune to go to, in order to feel something and then die.)

So the day my husband, Brad, asks me if I'd like to go on a wellness retreat at a spa town just outside of Rome, I surprise myself when my instant response is "Fuck, yes!"

We Are Experiencing a Slight Delay

To be fair, it's Italy—who would say no to that? But here's where the really perverse part comes in. This will be an alcohol- and caffeine-free, plant-based, gluten-free trip. So all the things one wants to go to Italy to enjoy—such as a bowl of pasta Bolognese with a glass of Chianti and espresso afterward—are off-limits.

It's like taking someone to Waikiki Beach and letting them enjoy it from inside a shipping container. What kind of sick mind concocts a trip to an Italian hill town in the middle of summer to chow down on chickpea frittatas and dandelion tea? The other things one would want to do in Italy—shop, eat gelato, and swim in the Mediterranean— will be replaced by a daily schedule comprised of four hours of hiking, three fitness classes, and a massage (the one slightly pleasurable activity is fifty minutes long, the length of a good cry).

I'll take any excuse, though, for a trip halfway around the world. To get me to go to a restaurant in downtown LA is all but impossible. The traffic, the parking—no, thank you. How good can chicken be? But an eighteen-hour travel day for a bowl of pasta I saw Antoni eating on Instagram and I'm in. I mean, if I'm going to leave the house I might as well go someplace good. One hour, twenty—it's all the same once you've closed the front door.

Besides, I have a plan. The wellness retreat Brad and I are to partake in will last one week, and will mostly involve, from what I can glean from their website, pain and starvation. Therefore, we will arrive in Rome three days early to eat, lie around, and eat some more. Three days of saying to each other, "Do you think you can eat again yet?" before heading out to our next plate of cured meats and cheese. Falling asleep as our last bites of gelato drip from our mouths and onto our pillows. After that, a week of root vegetables and seeds might not be all that bad.

I research restaurants beforehand as if I'm studying for the bar exam. It's exhausting, time-consuming work that includes, but is not limited to, Tripadvisor, Yelp, Eater, *Condé Nast Traveler*, *Bon Appétit*, several hotel concierges, friends, and finally my own instincts. Every restaurant is cross-referenced at least a dozen times. Normally, there is room for error, but on this trip, I cannot afford to broker any unwanted surprises. Each meal is precious.

Brad has no idea how many hours I spend on my research. It took less time to write this book. I make it sound casual, though. "Hey, check out this place," I say, passing my phone to him. "Looks good, right?" as I show him the menu of a restaurant I've already spent six hours vetting. I make it seem as if he has a choice in the decision-making, when the final picks are carved into my brain like the Ten Commandments.

I'm sure I have some sort of obsessive personality disorder that can be easily diagnosed. Perhaps they can look into it in Italy during one of my four-hour hikes, but I'm always happier not knowing. I prefer to think of it as a quirk instead of a diagnosable illness that should be medicated. I always marvel at the people who can go on vacation and just walk into any restaurant off the street, saying, "This looks good." (It's *not* good, by the way. You went to the wrong place—how does that not kill you?)

Early on in our twenty-two-year relationship, Brad learned how to tell when we were going to have to extract ourselves from a restaurant.

"Is this okay?" he'd ask tentatively as he slowly lowered his coat from his shoulders.

"Yeah, yeah, it's fine, it's great." But he could read my face like tea leaves, and knew that he should start putting on his coat again, and that we would be leaving.

One of my proudest accomplishments is knowing that over time, I have made Brad exactly like myself. You can't do it to someone if it's not already in there somewhere, but let's just say I brought it out and nourished it to its fullest potential. Now sometimes we'll be at a restaurant and Brad will say, "Come on, let's go," and I'm like, "Oh, I thought this place was okay." These are my happiest moments. If I have accomplished nothing else in my life, I have accomplished this. (If you haven't turned your partner into an exact replica of yourself after over twenty years together, well, then I don't know what you've been doing.)

Wellness

We never bond more than when we're sitting at the right restaurant, at the right table, having ordered the right thing. It's one of the few moments in life when I can exhale contentedly. If I were married to someone who was annoyed anytime I wanted to change tables, they would spend a lot of their life annoyed. To me, it's a sport, and I need a partner that approaches it with the same esprit de corps. The most self-restraint I ever show is when a friend picks the restaurant. "Is this place okay?" they ask as I swallow my misery with a pained smile that says I just stepped on a nail. "It's so cute."

I should say that these restaurants do not have to be the trendiest, or the busiest, or the most expensive. They just have to be "right." And it's hard to express just what the criteria for that are. I can't even put it into words, there are so many variables to consider. But let's just say, you know when it's *not* right. Fortunately, Brad and I can communicate telepathically now. An imperceptible glance between us has us both out the door within seconds. (We communicate the same way in choosing hotel rooms, but that will be covered in a later chapter.) If we were ever to separate, I don't have enough years left in my life to train another person properly.

Sometimes I feel a bit guilty for what I have turned Brad into. I mean, he *is* from Canada. How dissatisfied would he have ever been at any restaurant in, say, Paris, if I hadn't turned up to tell him why it was terrible? I don't think it's possible to undo the damage I've done to him at this point. (Although he was an all-too-willing student, soaking up information like a sponge. Now it's also not possible for him to go to any place in the world and truly relax, unless he knows he's at the right restaurant. I hate this place, he'll text me from Madrid or Miami or New York, and I think, smiling, *I made that.*)

The job of choosing restaurants in Rome is made trickier by the fact that this retreat is in August, the month when all of Italy shuts down. A difficulty level akin to running a marathon on your hands. To me, it would make more sense if the Italian people staggered their vacations: half take off July, half August. That alone would prevent the entire country from coming to a grinding halt for one-twelfth of the year. But nope, they all want August. And they get it. This leaves Italy populated primarily by sweaty Americans and Brits for an entire month. It's as if the country kept the door open and left a note that said, "Put everything back the way you found it."

A few viable dining options remain open, though. Once the list of restaurants is complete, I now find myself tasked with another, even more challenging, ordeal.

"Did you read the email from the retreat?" Brad asks.

"No," I say, "it was too long." And it was. I find it best to completely ignore any too-involved emails.

"Well, you have to read it," he says. "There's a lot of stuff we need to do."

"You mean, BEFORE we go? Isn't it going to be awful enough, once we're there?"

Apparently, we need a whole new wardrobe. The clothes we own are designed for sitting in cafés with our legs crossed as we sip cappuccinos, not for scaling the Apennines. I am to learn an entirely new vocabulary consisting of words such as "moisture wicking" and "hydration bladder." We are also supposed to break in our hiking boots for a month before we leave and start weaning ourselves off caffeine ten days beforehand. I'm not quite sure how one breaks in hiking boots if one doesn't hike. I won't lie: I'm starting to get a bit nervous. This will be my first trip to Italy that induces a panic attack.

I will say, the trip to the sporting goods store is not without its moments. Assuming the identity of hard-core hikers, Brad and I describe our trip, and the sales staff snaps into action. Suddenly, we are in a dressing room trying on shorts and shirts with the fabric of a trampoline, all magically designed not to be sweated through. Socks and underwear are produced with this same miracle fabric (not one you'll see walking a runway anytime soon) whose existence I was oblivious to only minutes before.

As we leave with shopping bags full of gear, I have a sick feeling in the pit of my stomach.

Brad asks, "You still want to go, right?"

"God, yes, don't you?"

"Yeah, of course. I think it's gonna be great."

"I do, too!"

We are both playing a dangerous game of chicken. Neither of us wants to pull the plug on something into which we are already too deep. There is an unspoken understanding between us that we will keep lying to each other until this is over. The more convincing the performance, the better.

"I actually can't wait to go," I say, upping the ante. "We're gonna be in the best shape of our lives. Thank you so much for arranging this."

"I'm so glad you're excited. I was worried."

Oh, good, he believes me. At this point, the truth will do no one any good. Besides, if you tell yourself something often enough, you can convince yourself of pretty much anything.

It is now a week before we leave, and we are supposed to be slowly cutting out caffeine. I decide I'll just wing it when the program starts. I'll be nursing a coffee until the moment I walk through the doors. If deprivation is the name of the game, I don't want a head start. Brad begins to eliminate caffeine on schedule, but eventually gives up, as I knew he would. We have three days in Rome before the retreat starts; what are we supposed to drink in the morning? Water? There is no more romantic sound in Italy than that of a porcelain cappuccino cup clinking against its saucer. A water jug thudding onto a starched tablecloth does not conjure images of *A Room with a View*.

Packing for the trip is its own mini-challenge. Both Brad and I refuse to check luggage (this topic, too, will get its own chapter later on; that's how important it is), each item must be given the utmost consideration before earning a coveted spot in my carry-on. (The most slovenly dressed people at the airport are always the ones traveling with the most suitcases. I don't get it. How many sweatpants do you really need to bring?)

Our time in Rome is a fever dream of carbohydrates and dairy washed down with extensive amounts of caffeine and wine. (The wine is only for me. Brad does not drink. He's been sober over twenty years. I love having a sober partner; it has prevented me from becoming an alcoholic.) Due to our time crunch, we end up choosing a pizzeria profiled in a Netflix series over a tour of the Vatican. I stand by our decision. (I saw the Sistine Chapel when I was twenty-two. When they start serving pizza, then I'll go back.) Out of the three restaurants I've curated for dinner, only one ends up being the right restaurant. The most celebrated of the three ends up being our least favorite. Because we have been so brainwashed by outside forces, it takes us a bit of time to admit to each other that we have not been won over. We ooh and aah over our first courses, but by the time we're shoveling in our spaghetti carbonara a hush falls over the table.

We Are Experiencing a Slight Delay

There is nothing as satisfying as realizing you and your partner both hate the thing that everyone else loves. Bonded by the knowledge that only the two of you are aware of the scam being foisted upon the rest of the world. Eater can go fuck itself. Our restaurant on night three in Trastevere (their East Village; it's adorable) turns out to be "right restaurant adjacent," so we give it a pass. After all, this is August, and ten Italians are running the entire country. In hindsight, we just should have eaten at the right restaurant three times.

We are both eerily quiet during the one-hour drive from Rome to the spa town where our retreat is being held. Neither of us wants to acknowledge that the next part of our trip might really suck. I haven't even mentioned yet that we will be part of a group of fourteen people. We will be participating in all activities and all meals as a group. I never even want to have dinner with another couple. I mean, I barely like Brad; what are the odds I'm going to like the other twelve people? Not good.

The problem is, I agreed to this trip three months ago, and three months ago, I didn't think it would ever be three months from now. (It's like when I got veneers on my teeth and the dentist said they'd have to be replaced in twenty years. I would have agreed to have my arm replaced in twenty years; that's how insanely far off into the future it sounded. He might as well have said the year three thousand

and fifty. Of course, now it *is* twenty years since I got them, and, well . . . fuck.)

The problem with being together for so long is that you can usually sense what the other person is feeling. You become like dogs, perceptive to the tiniest shift in emotion. I try to overcompensate for my dread by filling the car with nonsense chatter. *If I act normal, he'll think everything is fine,* I tell myself. And I can see him doing the same thing. I'm happy to talk about something, but I'm also happy to not talk about it. I mean, we're going; there's nothing we can do at this point, so we might as well pretend with each other that we're excited.

"It'll be good to give up caffeine for a week," I lie, gripping my latte cup like a life preserver.

"Yeah," he says, "it'll be like a reset."

"Exactly!" I agree, although what it is we're resetting is never quite clear. It's just something we've been saying for the last three months, when we need to remind ourselves why we're doing this.

We pull up to the spa hotel where the retreat is being held. It sits at the foot of a beautiful hill town dotted with restaurants and cafés that we are never to enter. (Like going to Chippendales on a night they don't take their clothes off.) We drop off our carry-on bags in our room (I manage to change ours to one with a terrace and a better view, putting the last minutes of my caffeinated high to good use), and are immediately led to an orientation session where we are offered herbal teas and lemon water by the wellness retreat staff. A group of Italian and American young people whose main purpose, we will soon discover, is to keep us constantly moving.

Our fellow retreat members sit around on assorted chairs and sofas as we are taken through what will be our daily routine. We discreetly glance at one another and exchange shy smiles, as if to say, *I'm embarrassed to be here, too.* I glance nervously at the large dining room table where I'm assuming we will be taking all our meals. The group is comprised of all ages. I'm relieved to see a man over sixty; at least I know I can outshine him.

Brad is instantly more friendly to everyone, walking over to shake their hands and introduce himself as I wave from my seat. I wasn't prepared for him to start running for office the second we got here. Already he's more popular and it's been five minutes. (The spasms of joy he goes into when he meets a fellow Canadian is almost too much to witness. You're both from a very unassuming country. Congratulations, now calm down.) As he joins me on the sofa, I give him a warm smile that says *That was so sweet*, and then it shifts a little and says *Great, now I have to introduce myself to everyone, too.*

Our first workout class is to begin as soon as the orientation is over. Followed by dinner, then sleep, then up at five thirty, then stretch class at six, then breakfast at seven, then a drive to our hiking location, then a four-hour hike, then lunch, then workout, then yoga, then a massage, then dinner, then bed. That's *one* day. Back home in LA, I can fill a day just going out to lunch. On the plus side, as a gay man I've been going to the gym for over thirty years; I think I'll be just fine with a workout class in Italy. Turns out I'm not.

As Brad and I walk back to our room that first night after a dinner of something green and red and mushy, I say, "I'm already having so much fun." He looks at me blankly. "Yeah, me too."

They call our room at 5:30 a.m. to wake us up. The voice on the other end of the phone has the energy of someone who has been up for hours cheering on cyclists in the Tour de France. Wellness people wake up very early, already operating at full potential. I don't know why their sleep patterns have to be so horrific. Can one not be well and wake up at 9:00 a.m.?

But I have decided to give myself over to this. I will be positive and upbeat and do everything that is asked of me without complaint. As I fill my hydration bladder (Google it) at the bathroom faucet (which they swear is drinkable) and put on my water-wicking outfit and un-broken-in hiking boots before the sun has even risen, I whisper, "So much fun," to nobody.

Now, I've been on hikes before; I do live in LA. But I have never experienced anything like this. It is a grueling four hours at a relentless pace. You know how when you're trying to pass someone on the sidewalk, and you speed up to triple your normal speed until you overtake them? Try doing that uphill, over rocks, for four hours. I feel like there has been a side conversation that I was not privy to. Everyone instantly seems to know that this is what we are doing, and we will not stop until it is over. I expected more of a strolling and chatting component, but this hike has a wholly unexpected competitiveness to it. A mere stop to tie your shoelaces is something that can send you immediately to the rear of the pack.

Eventually, over time, we are spaced out to such a degree that I don't see anyone else. Even Brad is far in front of me. We are equipped with radios, through which we can hear our guides egging us on as we keep an eye out for the tiny, intermittent orange flags that keep us on course. I am forever thinking I'm going in the wrong direction, until I see the tiny orange flag that is planted in the most difficult-to-see spot. I want to get on my radio and say, *Brad, thanks for fucking waiting for me*, but this does not seem like good form.

Both Brad and I have always been very independent. I just didn't expect him to ditch me in the middle of the Italian Alps minutes into our first hike. But good for him. I guess this is how he wants to play it. I'll die before I ever say to him, *I thought we'd be hiking together.*

Everyone on this trip is in way better shape than I had

anticipated, like they've all been in training for months. I am falling behind, now only two people ahead of the woman with a heart condition, by my count.

When we have been hiking for two hours, they announce a break for our apple snack. But I am afraid to stop. This break is my only chance to catch up. To get to that apple, I'd have to take off my backpack, and I don't think I could recover from that delay. I think I can hear Heart Condition rustling in the branches behind me, hot on my heels. I need to keep up this pace if it kills me.

Luckily, I'm able to suck water through the tube that comes out of my backpack (which attaches to the hydration bladder, in case you didn't Google it) without having to stop. Every time I daydream for even a second, I become panicked that I missed one of the tiny orange flag markers and am wandering off to my death. *HOW IS BRAD ABLE TO SPOT ALL THESE TINY FUCKING FLAGS?!* plays in my head on repeat. The relief I feel when I spot one after being certain I'm off the trail almost brings tears to my eyes.

It has now been hours since I've seen another person. I hope Brad is enjoying his new life at the front of the pack. It's not fair; I was in better shape than he was for the first ten years of our relationship. If I'd known then what I know now, I would've taken him on a wellness retreat in the Rockies right after we met, and left him crawling through

17

the muck while I led the charge without a care in the world. Instead, I'm the one scrambling to keep up, too afraid to lose even the one minute it would take me to get that fucking apple out of my backpack.

The chirpy guides cheer us on through the radio, reminding us to hydrate. *Shut the fuck up!* How is it possible that less than twenty-four hours ago, I was sipping a Bellini in the courtyard of the Hotel de Russie? Yet something propels me forward. Probably all the films I've seen of people in situations like this where something always propels them forward. I have, thankfully, been conditioned by Hollywood to survive this.

The four hours pass like a prison sentence. I arrive at the end of the hike (not last, thank God), where I see Brad with the rest of the group, waiting at the vans that will take us back to our hotel.

"You made it!" he says.

No fucking thanks to you. YOU LEFT ME! "Yeah, of course I made it," I respond with a chill in my voice that's imperceptible to anyone but Brad.

Five minutes later, the final two hikers appear. If I had stopped to even blow my nose I would've been last. The thought chills me to the bone. At least now I'm at the bottom of the middle of the end. Acceptable. Maybe. The guy in his sixties who I thought I'd be mopping the floor with was apparently in the military, so that sucks. Thank God one woman has a heart condition, or I'd be completely fucked.

In the van on the way back to the hotel, Brad says, "I can't believe you didn't eat your apple."

"I was saving it in case I needed to survive on it."

He smiles as if I'm joking. But I'm too tired to talk, or even complain about the radio that's playing too loudly. (All right, fine, I do ask to lower it. But just a little. I haven't had caffeine and I have a crippling headache!) I look at my phone. It's not even noon.

I walk back into the hotel, trying to hide the pain in my knees. Every move is orchestrated to make me look carefree and young. "So fun." I pick at my grain bowl and smile at my tablemates. "Yum." Brad happily chats with the group. Knows everyone's name. You'd think he was hosting a bridal shower.

I'm mentally steeling myself for the two fitness classes still to come. I get through them somehow. They keep you moving the entire day, so there's really no time to process the horror.

It's not until we are both in our room, preparing for bed, that Brad suddenly says, "I hate it here."

You could've fooled me, I think, but say, "Oh, thank God, me too, it's awful!"

We spend the next hour scrolling on our phones, looking

at hotel rooms in Capri and Portofino, planning an escape that we both know will never take place.

The next day is pretty much like the first day. And so is the one after that. And the hiking doesn't get any easier; in fact, it gets even more difficult. And I am now taping my knees every morning like professional athletes I've seen on TV documentaries. But the hikes are something that I must accomplish. We all must accomplish. I don't know why this is true, to be honest. I could just as easily hang up the phone when they call at 5:30 a.m. Could stay in bed. Go for a walk into the hill town we still haven't seen. Get a gelato. I do it, I guess, because we all are. And here is another thing that happens: I like the people in the group. They encourage me, and I them. They're kind of great, all of them. And we talk at dinner. Brad and I don't even sit together, most meals. It reminds me of maybe how I used to be; someone who would eat a meal with people he had just met.

Now, on the hikes, I know that Brad will be ahead of me, hiking with the others that are always toward the front. I am farther back, talking with whoever is nearby, always happy for the company—until inevitably someone pulls ahead, someone falls behind, and I am hiking alone again. I keep up the pace. When I hear the wellness guides come on the radio reminding us to hydrate, I do. When they cheer us on, I cheer back. I am part of a group. I don't know when this happens; maybe around the time my headaches stop.

Wellness

And every day, on every hike, this is what I listen for: from up ahead, if it's very quiet, I can hear Brad's laugh. He is sharing a joke with someone; I don't know what, I don't know who. He is easy with people, he is kind, he is present. This reminds me of what I've known for over twenty years. Underlines it. The feeling I get each day as I hear him. Knowing he's up there somewhere laughing. It makes me feel, well . . . well.

On the last hardest day, on the last hardest hike, I reach Brad and the others that had been so far ahead of me all week. They sit in the grass looking out over the view, eating their apples.

"I knew you'd make it," Brad calls to me.

I pull out my apple and join them.

chapter two

The Grill

I wasn't always a snob. (And am still actually not—except for when I am.) I was born in Queens. We are not known for breeding snobs. I mean, it's not like there's a fancy part of Queens where we all wished we lived. It's all pretty much the same: middle-middle-middle everything. The only rich people I knew were on television. They drank champagne and wore Nolan Miller gowns and lived in places like Denver or Dallas, not Flushing. I wanted to be rich, but in the way someone wants blue eyes when they have brown. There's really nothing one can do about it.

All the traveling I did as a child was on cruises because my father worked in sales for Cunard Line. These cruises were free and usually last-minute. Amazing how one day someone could be sitting in their ranch house on Twenty-Fourth Avenue, only to find themselves a day later sailing toward Bermuda on the *Queen Elizabeth 2*.

I first became aware of a "class system" as a child on board the *QE2*. This was a British ship, and we all know that if the Brits are good at one thing, it's dividing people according to status and bloodlines. Your class was determined by which restaurant you were assigned: Queens Grill, Princess Grill, Columbia, or Britannia. Queens Grill was first class; Princess Grill was business; Columbia economy plus, and Britannia was steerage. If you've seen *Titanic* (and you have), you know how this goes. We were *never* in the Queens Grill. Could never even get near it, as any of the areas for the upper classes were roped off. We were Britannia people. And proudly, I might add. I liked being of the common folk. We weren't Queens Grill people, and I didn't care in the least. This seems odd to me now, but it was true. I was happy just being on the ship; it would never have occurred to me to want more.

It wasn't until a Christmas cruise when I was in high school and my sister, Maria, was in college, that I was forced to reckon with our lowborn cruise status. My sister had an acquaintance from NYU that she unexpectedly ran into our second day on board. And he and his family were eating in the Queens Grill.

I had never even met another Queens Grill passenger

before, and now here I was face-to-face with a teenage one. When my sister told him we were eating in the Britannia restaurant, I felt embarrassed (not knowing why), but later masked it with defiance. "Who would want to eat in there with all those snots, anyway?"

This acquaintance of hers from NYU was a real little twat, too. Looking down on the swarms of middle-class passengers (that I was forced to look at now through different eyes). Making fun of the way they dressed, the way they looked, the way they talked.

I hated every time we bumped into him on board. Once you become aware of something you previously hadn't been, it's hard to go back. A person from the other world had crossed over into ours, and basically told us we were garbage. He could go anywhere, this NYU freshman. He had carte blanche. But my sister and I could not go beyond the velvet ropes with the dangling placard that read FOR QUEENS GRILL PASSENGERS ONLY positioned outside their little private bar, and restaurant, and theater balcony.

It all suddenly seemed horribly gross and unfair. Something I had never given a thought to was now all I could think about. What really went on in the Queens Grill, anyway? The shipboard stories were apocryphal: trays of lobster every night, caviar spooned out as freely as peanut butter, ordering food that wasn't even on the menu! It was Caligula's Rome, and suddenly I wanted in.

We Are Experiencing a Slight Delay

Late one night, my sister and I see him, this NYU freshman, as we wander the decks, not wanting to go to sleep. "It's so boring," he says, looking truly, painfully bored. And even though I am closeted, it is clear to me that he is gay. An unspoken current travels between us. Pinched and thin, dressed all in black, he disdains even the Queens Grill. "It's awful, everything is so tacky and cheap. I can't wait to get home." A dime-store Sebastian Flyte, without the charm or accent.

I'd never met anyone who was desperate for a trip to end. We follow him as he leads us through the ship, looking for entertainment. The rich are good at getting people to follow along. Their attitude of entitlement is a kind of power over those too stupid to recognize its vapidity. (People born rich always think they're smarter and cleverer than they truly are. Surrounded by toadies whose livelihood usually depends on the rich person's money, they are raised to think they're special, when in actuality they couldn't be more basic. It's just that there's no one who will tell them.)

We pad along behind him into the now-empty Queens Grill, already set with china for the following morning's breakfast service. "Come on," he orders, and we rush to keep up, taking in the room with a hushed reverence usually reserved for the Louvre. He leads us through the swinging doors into the kitchen, all gleaming stainless-steel cabinets and counters, everything in its own perfect place.

The Grill

My sister and I look nervously at each other as he pulls a cake out of the refrigerator as freely as one would at home. He cuts a slice, takes a bite, makes a face, and then drops his fork onto the spotless counter, spraying bits of chocolate everywhere. If he had bitten the head off a chicken, I couldn't have been more dumbstruck. But there was also something thrilling about it. Something exciting. Something that I liked. We leave, frightened of being caught, as he continues making messes for others to clean up.

It's not that what I had wasn't enough. It's just that now there was a little voice whispering to me, where there hadn't been before. One that said, *You're in the wrong goddamn restaurant, Mister.* I loved the Britannia people, I did. But now I loathed them a bit, too. This rich little twat from NYU had awakened something ugly in me. Something that now wanted more. More, more, more.

"I fucking hate him," I tell my sister, once back in our tiny cabin. "What an asshole."

"Yeah. What an asshole," she agrees.

But I am unable to fall asleep, my wheels already turning.

chapter three

World Cruise

I'm writing this on my birthday (March 22; if you Google me, the year is also cruelly displayed) because I feel that if I don't do it on my birthday, I never will. I'm not sure what this is going to be, but let's just see where it goes. Maybe it's kind of a companion piece to the previous essay. In any case, you'll only be able to read this if I finish it today. So if this is inside a book right now, hats off to me.

This thing happened to me about ten years ago that was kind of weird. Well, maybe it didn't *happen* to me; maybe I sought it out. But I didn't know it would end the way it did. I read that the *QE2* will be going out of service. Will be taking her final world cruise. I decide I want to travel on her one more time, and I find a segment of the cruise that is perfect. I will join the ship in Singapore, sail three weeks to Vietnam and Japan, across the Pacific to Hawaii, and then back to LA. My husband, Brad, is unable to join me, so I'm going alone.

It feels right to say goodbye to this part of my childhood, my youth. I had always wanted to do a world cruise on the *QE2*. The thing that cinches it for me is that in the middle of the Pacific Ocean, we will be crossing the International Date Line on March 22. Which means we will be gaining an extra day, so there will literally be *two* days of March 22. In what other circumstance does someone get to have their birthday two days in a row? Fate was calling, and I was flying to Singapore to answer.

My first indication that this is not going to be a dream trip should be when I show up at the dock, and the ship isn't there. Nor is there any representative from Cunard Line. I look around again, as if I've misplaced a bag. I mean, it's an ocean liner; it shouldn't be that hard to spot. Suddenly, I start doubting everything. Did I get the date wrong? The country? What am I now doing standing alone on an empty dock in Singapore with a suitcase full of jackets and tuxedos for formal nights? It's not like you could call the *QE2*.

I'm pretty much resigned to flying the fifteen hours back to LA, when a minivan pulls up and a man in a Cunard uniform lowers his window.

"Are you Gary?"

"Yeah . . ."

"Well, get in."

Apparently, I am the only passenger joining the cruise in Singapore and they have forgotten about me. I get in the minivan and am driven away from the passenger terminal into the container port, where massive cargo ships are loading and unloading huge crates. After twenty minutes, we unceremoniously arrive at the ship.

Stepping foot on board for the first time in many years is not unlike bumping into an old girlfriend (I say "girlfriend" because all ships are female). After the initial pleasantries, there's not much to say to each other. And then you start completely picking them apart. How did I ever date this person? A bit worn and tatty, and if I didn't know better, I'd say she was embarrassed to see me. But the open decks are still beautiful. The lines of the ship perfect.

I unpack in my Princess Grill cabin. I choose to dine in the Princess Grill (their business class, if you will) because it is the only room on board that is unchanged since her launch in 1969. I am assigned a table for eight, and the first night the only other dinner companions I have are a mother/daughter duo from England. The daughter is perhaps my age. Then again, it's always hard to determine the age of a Brit. Many a time I found out someone I previously thought was sixty was thirty. They don't age like we do. They're more like bananas.

We Are Experiencing a Slight Delay

Before I continue, I have to be honest. I'm stopping for today. I got distracted. Got a few phone calls, answered texts. I mean, it *is* my birthday. So, I think I'm going to continue with this tomorrow. I still don't know if there's anything here. Writing is like that sometimes. I will often say to myself—is this anything? But I'm not sure anything is anything. Not really.

I'm going to give myself another day (maybe two). Is that okay, or did I break the contract of the first paragraph? Am I, like, an unreliable narrator? Remember learning about that? I do. I remember being fascinated with the thought of an unreliable narrator. And now I am one.

More tomorrow. I'm going to have a shrimp cocktail and a cheeseburger tonight at Craig's in West Hollywood. I hope it comes out well done, or else I won't be able to eat it and will have to send it back. (I'll let you know if anyone sings "Happy Birthday." I'll die if they do. Also, I'm going to eat all my fries and drink wine. I feel like you should know that.)

Okay, it's March 23 now, birthday over. First off, my cheeseburger *was* well done and perfect. (I always have to cut it in half and make sure there's no red inside, or else I can't eat it. It's very stressful for me because if it is bloody, I have to send it back, which means I will inevitably be eating alone because everyone else will have finished their dinner by the time it returns. It makes for an unbalanced evening.)

Second, there was not exactly singing involved, but a huge ice cream/cake-y dessert arrived at the table with some sort of firework in it that caused the entire restaurant to turn and look at me for the duration of the firework. And as I desperately tried to blow it out, my friend John Benjamin Hickey (isn't that the best name you've ever heard?) took a picture to send to Brad, who is working in Canada. Apparently, you can't blow this stick-of-dynamite-looking thing out, because it's some kind of sparkler and just has to run its course. Which is kind of worse than singing. If anything, the singing would have made it better. Something to fill the air, other than me desperately trying to blow something out that was not meant to be blown out.

I was too stressed to think of a proper wish, so at the last second before it went out, I just went with something lame like "good health." I also did not order this dessert. I don't know where it came from. I think it was sent, which was very nice, but I didn't get the dessert that I ordered. Which was the one that I wanted. But it would have seemed churlish to ask for it, at that point.

In any case, Brad posted this photo on Instagram that John took of me trying to blow out the dynamite. Brad wrote on it, "This makes me so happy." And I was thinking, *Does this make you happy because you know it's my worst nightmare? Or do you think I'm enjoying this, and that's why you're happy?* After twenty-two years together, either scenario was problematic

in its own way. I saw the photo and thought I looked terrified (which I am). But maybe I just looked like a normal
person with a birthday dessert in front of them.

I don't know where I got this visceral aversion to having
people sing "Happy Birthday" to me, but as I think about
it now, I'm pretty sure it was passed down from my mother.

When I was around twelve, my family went on a cruise to
Bermuda. The last night of the cruise fell on my mother's
birthday.

Every day leading up to it, there would be several birthdays in the dining room, each one accompanied by a group
of waiters and friendly passengers joining in a rousing chorus of "Happy Birthday." And each night my mother made
us promise not to do that.

As her birthday got closer, her warnings got more in-
tense. "If you have them come and sing for me, I swear
to God, I will walk out of here." It got so bad we started
getting stressed when strangers were being sung "Happy
Birthday" to. *She's not gonna like that*, I'd think, looking down
at the floor.

On the night of her birthday, per her instructions, we
had no birthday cake. By this point, I was practically afraid
to even wish her a happy birthday. And as we were leaving
the restaurant, she didn't talk to any of us. Clearly, she was
upset by something. I couldn't imagine what it was. When
one of us, I don't remember who, mustered the courage

to ask what was wrong, she responded, "I just didn't want them to sing. You could've gotten me a cake."

So I think I absorbed that and carried it with me. Now the idea of being sung to seems as horrifying as accidently cutting off your hand while chopping wood. For years, I thought my mother had overreacted, until I quietly and un-knowingly became her, often requiring those around me to possess the same mind-reading skills. Yes, we *should* have known, Felicia; just cake, no singing, one tiny discreet can-dle. Sorry, forty years later.

But back to now: I had an otherwise perfect birthday dinner. You know, as perfect as birthdays can be. Because let's face it, we are all my mother on our birthdays. Nobody wants too much fuss, but everybody wants *some* fuss. And it is up to those around us to ascertain exactly what that entails, even when we ourselves don't know. You are basi-cally setting your loved ones up for failure each year. "I just didn't want them to sing," indeed.

Now, you might have forgotten what this essay is actu-ally about (as have I). I just read it from the beginning, and will now get us back on track. I'm pretty sure how all of this links together. If not, I'll delete it all at the end. You might be reading this while doing something else, in which case your attention span is shot, and I don't have to worry about any of this stuff connecting. But for anyone who's focusing on this, I started this essay by writing about taking a segment of the *QE2* world cruise over my birthday. Do you remember? Don't go back and read it—it's fine. We cross the International Date Line on my birthday, so it will last two days. That's all you need to know. Had I finished writing this yesterday (as was my promise to you, if you recall), the flow would most likely have been better. But then we would not have had the story of my mother on *her* birthday. (And quite honestly, I might never have even thought of it. Funny how that works.)

So I'm back on board the *QE2*. (I'm in my forties, if I didn't mention it earlier. If I did, you most likely would have forgotten it by now anyway.) And I have dinner each night in the Princess Grill with a mother and daughter from England. (I insulted all Brits earlier, sorry.) We are seated at a table for eight, but for some reason, only three of us are ever at dinner together. (There is one man in his nineties traveling alone, wheeling his oxygen tank beside him, that I see leaving our table one night as I'm arriving, but other than that, each night is just the three of us: mother, daughter, and me. Not the threesome I was hoping for.) Since they are British (I'm about to insult them all again, sorry in advance) and are completely emotionally shut down, each conversation is about as easy as passing a kidney stone. (My editor is British, I just realized—uch, I hope you have a sense of humour [I even spelled it your weird way], Jonathan.)

In order to make it bearable, I have to lubricate myself with alcohol each meal. I get a bottle (okay, two) of
champagne for the table each night, like I'm fucking Jay
Gatsby. A few glasses in, and we're having a grand time.
I'm hanging on every word about daughter's work friends
and mother's gardening club, as if it's the series finale of
The Sopranos. And they're lovely people, they are. I just
don't want to be their hostage each night for three hours.

I skip dinner one evening and have it in my cabin after
a long day wandering Ho Chi Minh City (remember, this
trip started in Singapore). The next night, daughter is very
chilly to me. She behaves as if I had deliberately missed
dinner in the dining room so as to avoid having to eat with
them. (Which I did. But still, she doesn't know that.) So now
I have to work overtime in order to win them back. Which I
don't even want to. At this point, I'm at least twenty bottles
of champagne into them. One evening I try not to order
one, opting instead for a ginger ale. But if I don't drink,
they don't drink. I am the ringmaster of this tiny circus. I
make the decision to be an alcoholic for three weeks; I can
think of no other way to get through these dinners.

To make matters even worse, there is another mother/
daughter duo eating in the restaurant at a table for two (like
normal people) who I become friends with. I begin meeting them, and a charming older married couple, for a drink

in the restaurant's bar each night before dinner. Now the original mother/daughter become jealous of my relationship with this other mother/daughter. One night I eat with my new mother/daughter friends and it's heaven. We laugh, we toast, I really like them. But I can feel the daggers that *my* mother/daughter are glaring at me from across the room. I have been caught having a mother/daughter affair. I'm not sure why I don't just leave their table permanently. I guess it feels like it would be unkind to leave them alone. Me who gets them drunk each night on free (at least for them) champagne. Without me, they glumly poke at their food, barely saying two words to each other, but when I'm there, it's Carnival. For people who repeatedly insist they don't usually drink this much, they sure know how to knock 'em back. (Don't worry, I won't say anything about Brits and excessive drinking, Jonathan. Even though we're all thinking it.)

The cruise isn't quite turning out the way I had anticipated. The days in port are separated by long, lonely days at sea. I walk the decks, I go to the gym, I read. My childhood memories of the *QE2* now being replaced by these new, odd ones. A bit of melancholia has started to creep in. And the thing that had most excited me about this voyage now fills me with an unspeakable dread.

Once we leave Osaka, Japan, we will be at sea crossing the Pacific for six straight days—two of which will be my birthday. One birthday in and of itself is enough to deal with, but two March 22s in a row now seems like one too many. You know that feeling you have on your birthday where you're supposed to feel special, but you don't, and instead you feel a little sad because nobody's actually making you feel special—because, let's face it, other people's birthdays are a bore. We only care about ours. And then when it's ours, we realize it sucks because nobody else cares about it. It's a vicious cycle.

I usually spend most of the day making a shit list of those who didn't wish me a happy birthday. Then it's kind of waiting for it to be over, and then feeling terrible when it *is* over, because I didn't feel special. Not really.

And now on this cruise, I'm supposed to wake up, Groundhog Day–like, and repeat it again. In the middle of the ocean. With two mother/daughter duos competing for my attention. I don't think I have it in me. Six straight days crossing the ocean is a lot of champagne. I already feel like I'm going to have to attend a meeting when I get home. The pressure of having to entertain my table each evening is starting to eat at me. And daughter clocks even my slightest shift in emotion. Each time I have to rest my smile muscles, she takes it as a personal slight.

Or maybe I am just telling myself this; maybe it's all me and not her. Maybe I have cast myself in this role, and now it's the only one I can play: the sparkling dinner companion, always with the right anecdote, the thoughtful question, the concentrated look of feigned interest. Sprinkled with a smile, a laugh, a nod. I'm giving a better performance in the Princess Grill as "dinner companion to British mother and daughter" than any of the shipboard entertainers performing in the main lounge. If there's anything sadder than a gay guy with Broadway aspirations relegated to the chorus of a cruise ship musical revue, well, I haven't seen it. I was hoping there'd be at least one cute dancer I could cultivate a romantic obsession with over the long Pacific crossing, but nope, not even that.

If I want to make a move, I'm going to have to do it fast. I decide to depart the cruise in Osaka. I have never done anything like this before. The thought of leaving a cruise midvoyage is antithetical to everything I have stood for my entire life. As a child, I would become depressed knowing that eventually I would have to leave the ship. Now I'm depressed at the thought of staying on it.

After I make all the arrangements, I am suddenly giddy. I tell my mother/daughter at our last dinner that I have been called away for work, and will be departing the ship the next day in Japan. Daughter seems to find my excuse suspect, but, really, what sane person would abort a world cruise midvoyage, just to avoid another meal with their tablemates? Even she seems to think this is too far-fetched a scenario. It casts a bit of a pall over the evening—one that is removed with a few final bottles of champagne. I go out with a bang.

I disembark the *QE2* for the last time on a gloomy day in Osaka. My final glimpse of her is from my taxi driving away from the pier. She is obscured mostly by clouds, a ghost that literally just disappears. I take the bullet train to Tokyo, a city I have never been to previously. My plan is to stay a few days, and then fly back to LA the day after my birthday. I don't want to fly on my birthday because that's almost as bad as having it last for two days in the middle of the ocean. And if I fly home the day before my birthday, I won't have enough time to see Tokyo.

I'm not going to tell you about my time in Tokyo. It's fabulous; go. I'm going to skip ahead to my last night. My birthday. I'm having dinner alone in the hotel restaurant, reading my book, when a group of waiters appear with a birthday cake singing "Happy Birthday." I'm horrified; how does anyone here know it's my birthday? But then they pass me by and stop a few tables away from me. Singing to a woman who seems pleased as punch.

I return to my book as the restaurant empties for the evening. A few minutes later, I hear it again, a group of waiters singing "Happy Birthday." This time, they are headed directly to me, sitting alone in a half-empty hotel restaurant. I guess they knew from my passport. As they sing to me, I plead with them to stop. Confused, they awkwardly finish and back away as I quickly blow out the candles. I sit there picking at the cake and don't know why I'm crying.

Weeks later, once back in LA, I get a card from Honolulu from the other mother/daughter duo. The daughter writes that the crossing was beautiful. Sun each day; the ocean like a lake. That I was missed. And she encloses the ship's Daily Programme from March 22. In it, I'm named along with several other passengers. We are singled out for having our birthday two days in a row. Something so unique. Something so special.

chapter four

How to Eat Alone at a Restaurant

When I was a kid, I never had anyone to eat lunch with. I'm not telling you this so you'll feel sorry for me (I mean, it was like over forty years ago; I'm fine). I'm just telling you because it was true. Every day in high school, I would go to the cafeteria to buy a packet of chocolate chip cookies, and then eat them alone in the library while reading a Stephen King novel. It was a kind of heaven: safe, cocooned in my little cubicle. Yes, it would have been nice, I suppose, to sit at a table with the other kids, eat our sandwiches together, and talk about whatever teenagers talked about. I didn't know then and I don't know now. All I ever wanted to talk about was *One Life to Live* or *All My Children* or Broadway.

My life in my head was an adult life fully formed. I walked the halls almost outside of my body. As if Dickens-like, I was visiting my younger self from some future time, looking at fifteen-year-old me through a thirty-year-old's eyes. My youth an embarrassment, a hindrance, a curse.

Now, of course, when I look in a mirror, it takes me a good ten minutes just to find someone who resembles thirty-year-old Gary. Fifteen-year-old Gary's face is now many faces removed. Like the rings on a tree, you'd have to count a lot to go back that far.

So funny that I always wanted to be older. Even when I first started writing for TV at twenty-eight, I was afraid I looked too young to be taken seriously. I'd love to slap twenty-eight-year-old me hard across the face and tell him to knock it off! I should have spent each day just looking at my thick, wavy black hair, marveling at my eyelashes and eyebrows—fuck writing! Wanting to be older for my entire youth was a perversion that I am being punished for today. This fifty-something's mask I wear is God's way of saying, *Happy now?*

Back in that high school library, breaking off pieces of cookie as I read *Salem's Lot* or *The Stand*, I was ticking off the days of my youth like a prison sentence. Each one thrown away as carelessly as a tissue. But I was also preparing myself, unknowingly, for a life spent sitting at various restaurant counters with books, and eventually a phone, as my only dinner companion.

Learning how to eat alone at a restaurant is kind of like sex. You have to start with what's comfortable for you. Sitting at a counter with a book is, more or less, heavy petting. Third base is sitting alone at a table with a book or your phone. Sitting alone at a table with nothing at all to look at, well, that's fucking. It took me a long time to work my way up to that. I was always comfortable at a counter. Sitting alone at a counter is like saying, *I'm not a complete loser. I might be waiting for someone, I might be in and out fast, I might want to chitchat with the bartender.* Nobody at the tables is really clocking who's sitting at the bar, anyway. Nobody is really aware of who is alone, who is with a friend, who is just grabbing a drink.

But sit by yourself at a table as the waiter clears the extra place setting, and people notice. *Oh, I guess nobody else is coming,* they think. You are suddenly an object of pity and curiosity. What could this person have possibly done in their life that would prevent every other human being they know from wanting to dine with them? Why don't they just stay home so we don't have to look at them? Or at the very least, eat at the counter, where they'll just blend in. But alone at a table for two? People are talking. Sometimes even giving you a friendly nod that implies *good for you*, as if you had just scaled a rock cliff instead of opening a menu.

Brad can be quite sensitive. When we first started dating, he would become emotional when he saw people dining alone. Once, he was brought to tears by a woman in her sixties who did nothing more than sip her wine and smile contentedly.

"I feel so horrible for her," he was barely able to get out.

"Why? She's having a perfectly lovely evening."

"No, she's not. She's all alone."

"Yeah, and she wants to be alone."

"She just looks so sad."

"She's eating a roast chicken. She's on her third glass of wine. She's fine."

"Maybe you're right," he says, unconvinced.

"I feel like what would make her sad is knowing you were crying at the sight of her," I tell him.

"I never thought of it like that," he says. "But it still makes me sad looking at her."

"Then don't look at her!"

I never feel sad when I see someone eating alone. In fact, I usually want to trade places. But it did take me a long time before I would move from the counter to a table. Perhaps it was fear of all the Brads out there. Kindhearted souls who thought the only reason someone would be eating alone was because they had been shunned by their community, like an Amish person caught listening to the Top 40.

Once you commit to sitting alone at a table, you're really committing to proving to the entire restaurant just how self-reliant and unbothered by others' opinions you really are. You are on total display—you might as well be sitting there nude. Each trip to the bathroom is akin to Hester Prynne's walk through town with the scarlet *A*. All eyes are on you. Head tilted up, defiant, you walk slowly. Let them all get a good look. Here, here is the person that dared to sit alone for an 8:00 p.m. reservation! Do your worst!

I worked in London for a year in my forties. During this time, I moved from the conviviality of the counter to the solitude of a table set for one. I had been eating most of my meals out and had already been seated at every counter in town. I don't know why I hadn't been ready to go "all the way" up until this point, but I always have been a bit of a tease. I guess a counter implied I was just popping in to grab a bite, I'm a businessman on the go, busy busy, that sort of thing. But at a table, you have agreed to slow it all down. You want the full experience. To wallow in your oneness.

And oh, how wonderful that can be! No waiting until the other person is ready to order, nobody to count your cocktails (well, maybe the other diners, but nobody you know), no hearing about your dinner companion's job or kids (I've never really paid attention when anyone has told me anything about their kids, truth be told. Not until they went to college and could finally do something interesting).

When eating alone, you can sit with your own thoughts. Casually people-watch. (Just don't accidentally lock eyes with anyone. See Hester Prynne above.) Dispense with the charade of splitting a dessert. (I'm eating alone; of course I'm getting dessert!) Chat with the waiter. (Yes, sometimes as a party of one, you are forgotten, and a desperate attempt to flag down your server becomes a tragic kind of dinner theater for the other tables. It can't all be sunshine and rainbows.) I don't know why I didn't sit alone at a table earlier. A table all to yourself. It's like having a hotel room all to yourself, versus sharing it with another person. There's so much more room to spread out!

Doing it once was the hard part. Now it's fun: a night out with me. A book, a phone, nothing. As long as there are French fries and a glass of wine. Some stranger maybe to share a smile with. To be alone and not alone at the same time. That is the trick. Sometimes, though, there are the rare moments when I am brought suddenly back to my high school library, breaking off a piece of my chocolate chip cookie, crumbs on my book. And I have to shake it off and remind myself that that time is long past. That me no longer exists. Right?

chapter five

London: The Bus

I'm nineteen when I go to Europe for the first time. I audition for a summer acting program to be held at Oxford University and am accepted. (I write a bit about this in my first book, *Do You Mind If I Cancel?*, in the essay titled "Patti LuPone." Go get the book, read it, and then come back. I'll wait.)

I wish I could show you the passport photo that I had taken just after I turned nineteen. Sometimes I look at it now when I need a little lift. Look at it too long, though, and it has the opposite effect. (I'll bring it with me when I tour with this book, and you can ask me to show it to you. You'll tell me if I'm exaggerating.)

We Are Experiencing a Slight Delay

I had left the country before this, but only to the Caribbean and Canada, and at that time you didn't need a passport to get into either place. I'm pretty sure I didn't have photo ID, either. I think maybe my college meal card had a photo; could *that* have gotten me into Canada? It's quite possible. Traveling was much simpler in many ways, sorry to tell you. You could waltz onto an airplane with pretty much anything you could think of. I mean, we smoked on planes, so nobody was all that fussed about much. You could chop wood at your seat if you wanted. Friends could walk with you right up to the gate. If you were a smooth enough talker, you could probably even get on board. Security was basically someone you waved to.

And people actually wore pants and belts and shoes in airports. Today they come dressed as if for a sleepover or extended hospital stay. No fastener more complicated than a drawstring. Lugging pillows and stuffed animals, flip-flops lazily slapping the terrazzo floor. People paint houses in nicer clothing. Airplanes used to have a sense of occasion about them, but now they're nothing more than giant sleeping bags. They should just rip out all the seats at this point, throw down a pile of blankets, and call it a day.

But then, at nineteen, going to the airport alone to fly to London, I can think of nothing more glamorous. I wear the same striped button-down Ralph Lauren shirt that I'm wearing in my passport photo. (Again, just ask, I'll show it to you. I'm stunning.) I will be gone for six weeks; the longest I have been away. And I am more excited than I have ever been before. Walking through first class on my way to economy, I marvel at the spacious seats as I make my way to the back of the plane. (By today's standards, these same seats would be considered incredibly shitty and probably cause a riot among passengers. But back then, a seat that reclined eight inches was the height of luxury. This is one way in which the present has mopped the floor with the past. Now when I fly, if I don't have a business suite that's roughly the size of a Manhattan studio apartment I'm pissed.)

I'm seated among several other young people from the program, and we all become instant friends in the way young people do. Too stupid yet to be selective, we cling to each new person as if we'd just been released from solitary confinement (which, come to think of it, after my wasted lonely years of high school, I had).

When we land in London, I think, *This is where I'm supposed to be.* I don't know what this is based on; years of watching PBS maybe, or my father working for a British cruise line. All I know is, these are my people. Maybe it's the accent. Or the men's gorgeous flopsy hair (that they all lose by the time they're thirty-five, leaving a few scant, wheaty threads to cover the now-sun-blotched head). Or Julie Andrews. In any case, I feel instantly at ease. But we do not stay in London;

we are immediately transferred to coach buses that take us to Oxford. There, we are to be housed near Balliol College, where our classes are to be held.

I'm not going to talk about my time in Oxford, because the title of this essay is "London." Also, again, I kind of talked about this in my first book. But I didn't mention this part. After a week or so of acting classes, we take these same buses back into London for a trip to the theatre. (I'm using the proper British spellings for this essay. Jonathan [my British editor, remember?], will you please let me know if I have missed anything? I want to get this perfect. I know how you people are.)

All of the students are going to see Shakespeare's *Richard III*, starring Sir Antony Sher, at the Barbican. All except me, that is. Now, if you Google Antony Sher's *Richard III*, you'll see that it is one of the most hailed performances in theatre history. Even at that time, it was impossible to get a ticket, and the performance was already the stuff of legend. Antony Sher goes on to have an incredible career, but nothing eclipses this moment. (You really need to Google this to see that I'm not exaggerating. People still talk about it.) But I have other plans. I have decided instead to see *Starlight Express*, the Andrew Lloyd Webber musical that takes place entirely on roller skates.

"Oh, you can have my ticket," I say to whoever, on the bus ride to London. "I'm seeing something else."

"What?" my roommate David asks, surprised.

"*Starlight Express*," I say proudly.

He looks at me like I've lost my mind. "*Starlight Express?*" he repeats uncomprehendingly.

"Yeah, I decided to skip the other thing."

At nineteen, I wasn't a particularly discerning theatre-goer (it looks weird spelled like that, Jonathan), and a new Andrew Lloyd Webber musical was not something I was going to let pass me by. Now, I'm no snob—I love Andrew Lloyd Webber—but even the teenagers on that trip knew this was going to be a piece of shit.

That night, I sit in the last row of the mezzanine (I'm sorry, the Brits don't call it a mezzanine)—I sit in the last row of the dress circle (ugh) next to a dozing Japanese businessman, as actors on roller skates whizz by along dangerously raised platforms. They are supposed to be a train. A singing cat is one thing, but a singing train car is quite another. Each song as un-Memory-able as the last (I couldn't resist). The show becomes famous for the massive amount of injuries suffered among its cast. Actors slamming into each other like bumper cars, rolling off the stage and into the orchestra pit almost nightly. It is quite literally a train wreck. Today this would no doubt be shut down within the first week of previews, but in the '80s, you fell, you broke your wrist, you got up, and you kept fucking roller-skating. For that reason alone, I should have loved the show. But nobody breaks any bones the night I see it, unfortunately. At least that would have given it a bit of pizzazz. The Japanese businessman wakes up during the finale, and I give him a look that implies, *You didn't miss anything*. I couldn't tell you what it was about then, or now. Dissolved as quickly as cotton candy.

I meet my other classmates back at the bus that is going to take us out of the city. They excitedly talk about *Richard III*, and how Antony Sher's performance has inspired them. They are true artists, and I am the common trash from Queens who went to see *Starlight Express* instead of the theatrical event of the decade. I should have gone with them. I should have seen it. I should have shared in it. I decide that I will never miss something again that will nourish me, over something sticky and hollow.

I sit next to my roommate David on the ride out of London, back to our little house in Oxford. He is so excited and energized by what he has just seen; perhaps more so than anyone else in the group. He asks me how my show was, and I lie, saying I liked it. Feeling dumb for having missed what I should have seen, where I should have been. My first night in London could have been so special. A performance I might think of even now, all these years later. (A few nights after this, I see Ian McKellen in *Coriolanus* at the National. I still remember that performance, so all is not lost. Shakespeare wrote that one, too, by the way. It's okay you didn't know that. It's not a top ten of his, by any means.)

But also on this night on the bus leaving London, as everyone is talking and excited, I do something I have never done before. I rest my head on David's shoulder and fall asleep there for the whole ride. He does not stir; he lets me sleep until we arrive back at the house we all share. This is the first intimate moment I've had with a friend in my entire life. It's nothing, really, other than sleeping briefly on someone's shoulder. And it's everything. It's the only memory in this essay I'm positive I've gotten exactly correct. It's the reason I wrote it.

chapter six

London: The Covent Garden Hotel

When I'm twenty-five, I get a job as a front desk clerk at the Paramount Hotel in Times Square. I eventually become a bellman and spend a good chunk of my twenties hailing cabs and schlepping suitcases. Some of the rooms so small, when I would swing open the door, it would send the nightstand flying. The answer to any and all complaints was always, "This is New York." Too loud, too dirty, too small, too expensive. "This is New York." The implication being we don't give a fuck. Really, what did you expect?

We Are Experiencing a Slight Delay

It's not Singapore, where it's illegal to chew gum, or Switzerland, where you can eat off the street. People shave on the subway, for Christ's sake.

I would say "This is New York" with a smile and a little shrug at least a hundred times a day. And, really, what could they say after that? Whether you were scammed by a ticket broker or your husband was knifed in Hell's Kitchen, a shrug and a "This is New York" would fit the bill. I can't think of any other city in the world with an equivalent get-out-of-jail-free card. We were responsible for nothing. Any complaint was in the hands of a force far greater than our own. Room service could deliver a tray filled with human feces, and if you called down to the front desk, the response would still be, "This is New York." As if, what did you think was going to happen when you ordered room service? Any horror was made instantly explicable just by saying those four words.

I was often called to rooms in the middle of the night, only to be greeted by a naked guest with a hard-on. Even I thought, *This is New York.* (Although technically these were not, in most cases, actual New Yorkers, but when in Rome, I suppose.) Really, what else was I expecting to find on the other side of that door? Someone wearing pants?

At the time, I thought I hated working in a hotel, but thirty years later, I realize I loved it. First of all, I was gorgeous: thick, long '90s black hair, a tight little body. Too bad nobody told me. I mean, I knew I wouldn't be young forever in theory. But, yes, now that I look back, I guess I *did* think I was going to be young forever. Mostly, I was just young when I was working in that hotel. You know, *young* young. You're definitely not *young* young for long; ten years at most, and that's nothing. *The Big Bang Theory* was on longer than that.

So, yeah, the *young* young part goes by really fast. *Young* young is when you can stay out all night drinking, and look the same in the morning. The second you do not look the same in the morning, you are no longer *young* young. You might still be young, but you are not *young* young.

Each day in the hotel began as if one were starring in a play. In the locker room, we would change from our street clothes into our trendy uniforms (I had mine tailored to within an inch of its life) and step into the lobby as if onto a Broadway stage. We, each of us, played a part: front desk clerks, bellmen, room service, guests. It was like we had all stepped out of our lives somehow and decided to take on these artificial roles. Life inside a hotel is not the real world. It is make-believe. We were not our real selves here. This was a heightened universe of decadence and glamour and luxury. Each night was an occasion.

At home, I lived in a sixth floor walk-up apartment with no bathroom sink. But at the Paramount, I played the role of young bellman—flirt, hard worker, and aspiring writer.

We Are Experiencing a Slight Delay

During my time there, I would carry the bags of many actors, writers, directors and think, *That's going to be me one day. One day I'm going to be in town for a meeting, or on location for a film, or appearing on a talk show, and I'm going to be the one staying in the hotel. I'm going to get to play the part of the guest.* The part that does not require you to change out of your uniform, Cinderella-like, at the end of each shift, get on the subway and return to your walk-up apartment, brushing your teeth in the kitchen sink.

Many years later, long after I have left the hotel, left New York, and moved to LA and become a writer, I get a TV show picked up that will require me to live in London for an extended period of time. In the show, titled *Vicious*, Ian McKellen and Derek Jacobi have been cast as Freddie and Stuart, longtime partners. And I have cast myself, finally, in the role of Los Angeles Writer Who Will Be Living in the Covent Garden Hotel.

I have stayed in the Covent Garden Hotel many times before, during my many trips to London, but we're talking six months here. This is a whole other ball game. If I'm being completely honest with myself, I think I may have developed this show just so I could live in a hotel. Like, *How could I get to live in my favorite hotel in London for free, for half a year? I know!* I'm not saying that's the reason I did this show. But I'm not saying it's not, either.

"Are you sure you wouldn't be more comfortable in a flat

of your own?" the studio asks me. "Yeah, the hotel thing is kind of a deal-breaker for me, so let's get that going, shall we?" So as part of my contract, while in London for the show, I will live in the Covent Garden Hotel.

The day I arrive, the exterior of the building is covered in scaffolding. It will only be for a few weeks, I am told. What's a few weeks?

No matter, I am in heaven. In short order, I know every employee in the building, swanning through the public spaces as if I'm in my own living room. My favorite waiter shows me to my favorite table, brings me my favorite drink. I come and I go; I say hello, I say good morning, I say good night. I linger at the front desk, I talk with the concierge, I have a drink at the bar. "I'm off to the gym!" "I'm off to work!" "I'm off to the theatre!"

"How was the gym?" "How was work?" "How was the theatre?"

My table is always reserved for me in the restaurant, the little drawing room all mine as I sip my wine in front of the fire. The TV show becomes almost a distraction from my role as favourite (the British spelling is intentional, Jonathan; don't flag it) long-term hotel guest. One that requires me to do nothing other than smile, wave, be charming.

My room is a dream. A complete and utter dream. Fabric on the walls, a tub and a little sofa, an electric kettle for tea. What more does one need?

We Are Experiencing a Slight Delay

Guests come and go, but I do not. This is my home. I pad into the lobby in my slippers and robe. Grab an apple off the front desk, pick through the newspapers, idly chat to Dylan or Nicky or Kara.

"In for the night?"

"In for the night!" I pad back up to my room.

This goes on each day, this heaven. Everyone knows me, and I know everyone.

"Are you joining us for breakfast?" "Are you joining us for tea?" "Are you having the burger tonight?"

"I am!" "I'm not!" "I think I will!"

My newspaper, my book, my phone. My props. As I sit as I watch as I say hello as I say good night as I say the sun's out as I say it gets dark so early as I say how was your day off as I say do you have an umbrella here's my umbrella I'm going to bed I'll see you tomorrow good night good night good night.

And it goes on and on and on. And after a few months, one day the room feels just a tiny bit smaller. Just a tiny bit tinier. And one Sunday when there is no job to go to, no work to be done, I find myself in my room, alone, wondering how I can get from my little shrinking sofa to the street without seeing another person. I realise (British spelling again intentional—which, by the way, I am required to do on every script for *Vicious*. I mean, it's not like you can see the script on TV, but whatever). I do not have another "good morning" left in me; it seems I have run out. I find myself suddenly empty. The reserve I keep for small talk, for smiling, for engaging with other people, while quite deep, is now depleted. I had clearly not thought this through. I did not know there would be a time limit on the role of "favourite long-term hotel guest." And I have reached it. To answer Barbra Streisand's gorgeously sung question, "Have I Stayed Too Long at the Fair?," fuck yes.

There is no route to get from my room to the street without passing at least half a dozen familiar faces.

They all know I'm in here; they're just waiting for me to leave, I would think, rocking back and forth in my room, the fabric-covered walls closing in on me. If I could have tossed the knotted bedsheets out the window and safely shimmied down the side of the building, I would have. But I am trapped in a room that has become the size of a thimble. The room *was* a dream, and that dream has become a nightmare.

It's nothing anyone in the hotel has done. They are all lovely, don't get me wrong. *It's not you, it's me,* I want to tell the hotel. Have you ever been in a relationship with someone, and one day woke up and realized (I'm back to American spelling at this point in the essay, Jonathan), *I don't ever want this person to touch me again?* Well, that's how I feel about the hotel. I don't want it to ever touch me again. I could pretend things were okay between us, but we will never be close again, not like before. It is as if a switch inside me has flipped.

Life inside a hotel is not the real world. And I want the real world back. I want my real life back. My dog, my husband, my bed, my home. But I still have a few more weeks left, and what was once heaven is now hell. (Like so many things eventually, if you get right down to it.)

"Everything all right today?" "Can we get you anything?" "Is something the matter?"

"I'm great!" "I'm great!" "I'm great!"

I consider checking into another hotel, one where no one knows me, in order to come and go in anonymity. But I don't trust myself enough not to just start the whole thing all over again. I stay the last weeks, I go through the motions, but my heart is no longer in it.

I get home, and a month later I receive an email from an employee I befriended at the Covent Garden Hotel. In it is a photo of the exterior of the building. The scaffolding, which had been up my entire stay, has finally come down. All these many months later. And it looks so beautiful. Like life inside those walls would be perfect.

I write back. "Please tell everyone I say hello."

chapter seven

London: Dinner with Maggie

I wasn't sure I was going to write about my dinner with Maggie Smith. (If you don't know who Maggie Smith is, just stop reading now.) But considering she's in *Harry Potter* and *Downton Abbey*, I feel like all ages between five and death are pretty much covered. It's not that I'm going to say anything negative, or will be spilling any tea. (I hope someone finds a copy of this book fifty years from now, and has to do whatever the future of Google is to find out what "spilling the tea" means. Every word we write hopelessly dates ourselves to future generations. Uch.) But this night keeps popping into my head every so often. I mean, I must be thinking about it for a reason, right? Maybe in writing this, the reason will reveal itself. Or maybe it won't. Maybe this will just be a brief essay about the night I had dinner in London with Maggie Smith and pitched her a TV show. Hopefully, that will be enough.

But let me go back a little. (I hate when people say "Let me go back a little." It's never a little. But *this* will be.) After my TV show *Vicious* has ended, a British producer I know, Barnaby, and I decide to work on a project in London together. One about an older married couple who are also a famous double act, who move into a retirement community for aging actors once their career dries up. We talk to Derek Jacobi, who was in *Vicious*, about starring in this, and he is on board. To play his wife, both Barnaby and I want Maggie Smith. But she has a reputation as being, well, mercurial. Just to get a meeting with her is proving to be quite difficult. She and Derek are longtime friends, though, so we decide to leave it with him. (Is this already more than going back a little? I'll go faster. You know what? Even better, I'll just cut to the dinner.)

I make myself completely available to Maggie. I am going to be in London for two weeks, and I'll be free any time she'd like to meet. Lunch, coffee, dinner, a drink, at whatever time would be good for her, wherever she would like—I'll make anything work. Through Derek, who is in contact with her people, I find out that she will think about it and let us know. And, after a week in London, suddenly, she does. She would like to meet for an early dinner at the Ivy Club (a private club; this is London, after all) at 5:00 p.m. I confirm that she would like to meet at five for dinner, and that this is the restaurant she'd prefer, and I'm told in no uncertain terms that this is correct.

I arrive early to meet with Barnaby, who has just gotten off an overnight shoot on another show he is working on. He looks really tired, and I'm already nervous.

"Are you going to be okay?" I ask.

"I'm fine," he says.

"Well, have some coffee. This is Maggie fucking Smith we're meeting."

Barnaby is a lifelong fan, too. *The Prime of Miss Jean Brodie*, *California Suite*, *Murder By Death*, *A Room with a View*: the list is endless. (Well, maybe not endless, but, you know, it's a great list.) I'm convinced I can sell this show to her once I pitch it, but I know it's going to require me to give a performance on par with one of hers. Fortunately, I will have Barnaby and, shortly, Derek as well, to assist. (Derek Jacobi, by the way, is one of the most brilliant actors in history. His performance as Claudius in *I, Claudius*—the *Game of Thrones* of its day—is one for the record books. But this essay is about Maggie; sorry, Derek.)

As of now, Barnaby and I are the only people in the empty restaurant. I don't know how I'm going to eat dinner at 5:00 p.m. I tell Barnaby we will let Maggie set the tone. Whether she would like to keep this just drinks or order dinner, we will follow suit.

Derek arrives, and now there are a total of three of us in the dining room. He's excited that she's agreed to meet. "This is a good sign," he tells me. Derek is the most lovely man alive, I should add. The three of us sit in a booth, strategizing.

"Have some coffee," I tell Barnaby, annoyed.

"I'm fine," he repeats, even though he looks like he just got out of that club in Berlin where people dance for three days straight.

At ten past five, Maggie arrives, looking like she would rather be anywhere else in the world but here. I stand to greet her and say something that fails to charm (that's the thing about having charm; when it fails you, it does so spectacularly).

She responds, "Why are we meeting here?"

"I thought you said you . . ." She stares at me, challenging. I recalibrate. "I'm sorry, I thought this would be a convenient place for us all to meet."

"Mm," she responds, uncertain. And I see that I have already failed the first test. She turns to Derek. "Who eats dinner at five o'clock?" *I sure as fuck don't.*

Derek gives me a look that says, *This is going to be tougher than I thought.* I see Barnaby (usually perfection with actors

68

of a certain age) stifle a yawn, and I want to reach across the table and choke him to death. If I could get a busboy to go out and score him a bump of cocaine right now, I would.

After several excruciating minutes of the most awkward small talk I've ever experienced, the waitress comes over to take our orders. We start with Maggie.

"What would you like?" the waitress asks.

"Nothing," she responds flatly, closing her menu. "It's too early to eat, don't you think? It's barely five," she says again to Derek, implying I was insane for suggesting this early hour. Then, looking around the room as if she'd just been dropped in an abandoned warehouse, "Where are we?"

We're at the restaurant you picked, at the time you picked, lady; that's where the fuck we are.

"Is anyone even hungry at this time?" she asks the table incredulously.

"I know I'm not," I say.

She orders sparkling water, and we all do the same. This is going to be a very short evening. We'll be done in time for me to go back to the hotel, shower, grab a drink, and still have it be too early to eat dinner.

Derek and Maggie are chatting, catching up, and I consider not even bothering with my pitch. What's the point? There's no way she's going to do it. But then I've always liked a challenge. And as far as actress pitch meetings go, Maggie Smith is Everest. I've already been gaslighted twice, and haven't had so much as an olive yet. I look at Barnaby for moral support, but he is dead behind the eyes. His exhaustion has gotten the best of him, and I can see that he's going to be of no use to me. The motherfucker.

I steel myself, and then I don't even wait for Derek and Maggie to finish talking; I just plow ahead. I begin telling her about my ideas, about her character, about the show. Maggie is clearly not impressed. She bats one idea away, then another, then another. But I am undeterred. I tell her why I think she's wrong. Then she tells me why she would never do this show. And I tell her why I think she should.

I see Derek looking at me nervously, but I forge on. I'm not going to go into the details of the pitch now, but let's just say I'm doing a good fucking job. I don't even look at Barnaby. I'll let nothing break my momentum. Maggie tells me this role is something that would be expected of her; it's something that she has done before, these comic roles.

I tell her that nobody can do them like she does. I cite moment after moment after moment of her career. Slowly, slowly, slowly, she is starting to soften. Then she snaps back into *No, no, no, I could never.* But I persevere, I tell her all the ways in which she could. Derek chimes in now; there is an opening, the history of this couple, bits they could do, who it reminds them of. And then she is smiling, even a laugh.

I talk, I talk, I talk, I talk. Every concern she has, I have a comeback for. Finally, she allows herself to say, "Well, if

I *were* to do this . . ." And she goes off on a tangent about something or other the character could do or say or wear. And now we are laughing, all of us, even Barnaby. The restaurant is filling up, and suddenly Maggie picks up her menu and says, "Shall we get a bite to eat?" All of us order dinner, a bottle of wine, and we settle in.

So this was always to be the plan. We'll see how it goes. Now it's beginning to make sense. The wine comes, we pour, we drink, laugh some more. Stories from her past, movie roles, stage roles, jealousies ("Everybody loves Judi"), loose-lipped now. Derek looks at me, giddy. *You've got her*, his eyes say.

A second bottle of wine. Was there a third? She looks at me then, unguarded, and tells me her fear. Reveals her insecurity. She is afraid she will be criticized for doing something she has done before. The comic, the joke, the clown.

It is at this moment that Barnaby yawns aggressively in her face. I kick him under the table, hard, but she does not notice. She is locked into me. We are locked into each other, and I realize what she is actually asking for is permission. Permission to do this role, one that fits so comfortably in her wheelhouse. And I tell her all the reasons why she should, and she looks at me, deep into my eyes, grabs my hand from across the table, and squeezes it. This private moment, just between us. We have made a connection. I have passed the final test.

Then we stop talking about the show. We gossip, drink, old friends now. Someone stops by the table to say hello, an actress that has known Maggie for years. Maggie looks at her confused, formal, nods hello back, a bit chilly. The actress excuses herself and returns to her table.

"Who *was* that?" Maggie says to me. "She just walked right up to the table like she knew me."

I was that actress a mere three hours ago, but now I am Maggie's coconspirator, her buddy, her pal.

"I have no idea," I say dismissively. (Even though I do know. I'll tell you who it was if we ever meet.) Barnaby repeats the actress's name to her. Maggie and I both look at each other and shrug.

"If you say so," she replies.

The evening winding down takes on the mood of a successful reunion between old classmates who do not want it to end. The plan is now for me to write the script, and then send it on to her agent. She hugs me goodbye warmly, and Barnaby sees her to her car. It's the least he can do.

Derek is excited. "She's in!" he tells me. "That couldn't have gone any better!"

We discuss next steps: where we would want to sell it, when we would want to film it. We say our good nights, will be in touch.

Barnaby and I stay a moment longer. The tension released, I let him yawn freely now.

London: Dinner with Maggie

"You did it," he tells me.

"Yeah," I say, allowing myself a moment to be pleased with the outcome.

Walking back to my hotel, as my head begins to clear from the wine, I have an odd feeling. And this feeling is confirmed when a few days later, back in LA, I receive an email from Maggie's agent. It was a pleasure to meet me, but she is not interested. There is no room for any kind of discussion.

I realize that my dinner with Maggie must have played itself out many times before, across the decades. I was just one in a string of countless others who had done the same dance with her. I imagine it played itself out in almost the exact way each time. Five-o'clock dinner, followed by "Who has dinner at five o'clock?" I should count myself honored that she found me entertaining enough to spend an entire evening with me. One where she could show me all her colors: haughty, acerbic, vulnerable, mischievous. Tell each well-practiced story as if it were a freshly tossed-off anecdote. Hit every highlight of her career. Her ups, downs, in-betweens. Turns out there was a show after all. And I was its only audience.

Now that this essay is finished, though, I'm still not quite sure why I keep thinking about that night.

chapter eight

Queen Mary 2

June
29

I'm in my hotel room in New York, the day before Brad and I are departing on the *Queen Mary 2*. We are traveling with my parents; his mom and her partner, John; and my sister, Maria, and niece Emily. I planned this cruise about ten months ago. I wanted my parents to have a vacation, since they haven't been able to travel in a few years. And this seemed like the perfect trip to do with both families. We'll be sailing to New England and Nova Scotia for a week.

My flight to New York was canceled three times. Finally, I took one with a connection through Detroit (that I barely

made) in order to make it to the ship in time. I had orig-
inally packed a suitcase (in a rare exception to my "only
carry-on luggage" rule), but after the three cancellations,
I eventually unpacked it and packed half as much clothing
in my carry-on (the universe was telling me to travel light
and be ready to run, and I listened). I can guarantee that
I'll be the only passenger boarding the *Queen Mary 2* with a
weekend bag.

We just got an email from Cunard telling us the ship is
going to be arriving in New York City late, so we will be
boarding at least six hours after our initial boarding time.
This is an inauspicious start. I don't even know how a ship
can be late; I guess the same way anything else is. It just
seems like something named the *Queen Mary 2* should be
expected to arrive on time, if nothing else.

Brad's mother, Debby, and her partner, John, have just
arrived at the hotel and we go down to the lobby to greet
them. I love to be the one to tell bad news first, so I am excited after their ten-hour car ride from Canada to get to tell
them the ship is delayed. I always look for the silver lining.
I guess I'm just a positive person.

We're waiting for them to get ready so we can all grab
a coffee. It always feels weird just sitting in a hotel room
midday, with nothing to do. I can sit at home for months
with nothing to do and not feel weird at all. But ten minutes

of sitting in a hotel room and I'm like, *What am I even doing with my life?*

We're going to see *Sweeney Todd* on Broadway tonight. Hopefully that's not delayed, too. I saw the original production for my thirteenth birthday. You'd think that would have given my parents a clue that I was gay and save me coming out to them ten years later, but no. The night we saw it, Angela Lansbury had just been replaced by Dorothy Loudon. (This is not as bad as getting Patti LuPone's understudy in *Evita*, but it's fucking close.) If Annaleigh Ashford is not in it tonight, I'm really going to lose my mind, I'll tell you that right now.

My goal for this trip is to not let any little things bother me and just have fun with our families. So far, a lot of little things have come up that could have bothered me, and we haven't even gotten on the ship yet.

Also, now I realize they have to unload thousands of passengers, clean the ship, then load up another couple of thousand passengers in the span of three hours. This doesn't even seem possible. I am expecting something really horrible tomorrow, so if it's anything less than really horrible I'll be pleasantly surprised. (Which is kind of how I think of every situation I'm about to go into.)

Oh, and after the show tonight I'm going to get a burger at the Polo Bar. I hope they remember to make sure it's well done, otherwise I can't eat it. But I promise not to let it bother me if it's not. Even though it will be really late and I'll be tired and hungry after the show.

Is there anyone I can call at Cunard so that the ship could maybe speed it up? (They gave us a twenty-five-dollar credit per cabin as an apology for the inconvenience. Is that a joke? Six hours is like half a day! Oops, I almost allowed myself to get bothered. No, no, no! But to be fair, the cruise doesn't start till tomorrow, so today I can still get annoyed by whatever the hell I want.)

More tomorrow from the ship. If we ever get on the fucking thing.

June
30

I'll start with the good news: the burger was well done. (Although, Brad, thank God, noticed that my burger had dressing on it, when I always ask for *no* dressing, and it didn't look well done—while his mother's burger appeared to have no dressing on it and to be well done. So we switched, and he was right, and everything was perfect.)

Annaleigh Ashford was in *Sweeney Todd*, as were Josh Groban and everyone else. The show was fantastic, and made me feel like I was thirteen again and watching it for the first time.

Now to the less-good news. Remember when I said I was expecting boarding to be really horrible? It was worse. It's after midnight as I type this, and I think the final passengers are just getting on board. That gives you some indication of the day.

We all met in Red Hook, Brooklyn, at the pier at 6:30 p.m. Along with three thousand other people. And maybe twelve chairs. I'd say the average age on this cruise is eighty-eight, so you can see where this would be a problem. Fortunately, my sister was with my parents, and they were already seated in three of the chairs. People were still disembarking the ship from the previous delayed cruise, so I knew things did not look good.

I tried to get some information from the two people that were working there. Poor things. I went up to the woman manning the "information" desk and asked her when we would be boarding. She gave me a look that said, *Do you really want to know?* Yes, I did. She said not for a while. I said that we were thinking of taking our parents for dinner in Brooklyn, and then coming back; did she think that would be a good idea? She said, "YES, GET YOUR PARENTS OUT OF HERE!"

I love real New Yorkers. There is no one in the world like them. No one. I knew to listen to her. So Brad and I gathered the group, and much of our luggage, and walked several blocks into Red Hook, where the fabulous hostess at the Red Hook Tavern got us a table for eight on a Friday night. I had one of the best burgers in New York City (sorry, last night's Polo Bar). Our first dinner on the cruise was on land, which seems kind of perfect, considering the last few travel days. And it was the best, most fun dinner. As Blanche Dubois would say, "Sometimes—there's God—so quickly."

We walked back to the *Queen Mary 2*. There was still a massive security line, although people were finally boarding the ship. But my dad is ninety-two, and he worked for Cunard Line from the time he was eighteen. He went into the navy for four years, and then when he got out, he worked again at Cunard until he was sixty-five. So this seemed like a particularly shitty homecoming to me. We were all in good spirits after dinner, but at a certain point, any sane human being has to go, "What the fuck?" But I promised myself I wasn't going to get annoyed by anything petty. On the plus side, this wasn't petty, so it didn't count. But here's the weird thing. It's the petty things that annoy me to no end and the big things I can usually deal with. I didn't think my dad was going to make it through the line at this late hour, and really the poor people working there were overwhelmed and doing the best they could with a bad situation. So I asked one woman if she could help me get through security with my dad, because I was worried with him waiting on the line. She directed me to her supervisor, Vincenza, who to me was perhaps the most perfect New Yorker I have ever had the pleasure of meeting.

I just looked at her and said, "My dad worked for Cunard Line since he was eighteen. He's ninety-two now, and this has been a lot for him, and I think we need to get him on the ship. Can you please help me?"

She looked me right in the eye and after a beat, said, "Bring him to me right now."

Quickly we got our whole party out of the line, and she got a wheelchair for my dad (who was grateful and needed it, and this perfect New Yorker saw that he needed it before I did), and she escorted us onto the ship. This is the thing about life. Sometimes one kind person can change everything. So today, instead of complaining and bitching and moaning, I am grateful. I'm grateful for Rebecca, the hostess at the Red Hook Tavern, who helped us when we asked for it. More than helped—treated us like favorite guests. Made us all feel at home. I'm grateful for Vincenza, who saved us. Who showed us a kindness that we needed.

I'm grateful for all the other people during the day who laughed and were patient and did their best. I'm grateful for my sister, Maria, and my niece Emily, for their constant positivity and help throughout the day. For my mother-in-law, Debby, and her partner, John, who is a chiropractor and helped my mom with the pain from her arthritis from sitting too long, waiting to board the ship. I'm grateful to my parents for showing me the love that they have throughout my life, and for being so excited to be a part of this trip and not complaining once about anything.

Most of all, I'm grateful for Brad, for being the best partner a person could have. For always being with me, by my side, smiling, working together to solve any problem. But especially today, June 30, the day when LGBTQ rights are being threatened by the latest Supreme Court ruling.

It's after 1:00 a.m. now. Brad is asleep. I think I feel the engines finally starting. I was so looking forward to watching us sail past the Statue of Liberty as we left New York. Instead, I'm going to take a Xanax and join Brad.

July
1

As I type this, I can hear the pianist playing in the Commodore Club, which is directly below our cabin. I think maybe it's Billy Joel. It's 11:30 p.m., so I'm guessing he stops at midnight? I can't see where it says an end time in the Daily Programme. I want to know who can still be in this lounge at 11:30 p.m., since my ninety-two-year-old father falls in the mid-age range of the ship's passengers. At this point, if they wheeled someone into the dining room in an iron lung, I wouldn't bat an eye.

I'm hoping this is the kind of background piano music I stop hearing after a while because I've become so used to it. But I'm also not the type of person who stops hearing something once they've heard it. In any case, this definitely falls into the petty department, and it's not something I'm going to allow to annoy me. Although I think most sane people would lose their shit. Anyway, who would I call? The captain? It's not like a hotel. Once you set sail, you're at their mercy. Do what they say and nobody gets hurt.

I'm guessing that Brad and I are the youngest people ever to have stayed in this cabin, and I'm in my midfifties. The only thing I can think is that all the previous inhabitants of this cabin, which sits directly over the Commodore Club's piano, had long ago lost their hearing, or at the very least had unplugged their hearing devices. There really is no other explanation, because I might as well be sitting on the other end of the piano bench. (Brad has already put his earplugs in and gone straight to sleep. It's like he's a college student, going into a dead sleep within seconds of closing his eyes.) The song the pianist is playing now is "What a Wonderful World." I really like this song, so for the moment this is actually quite pleasant.

Today we were at sea all day. We all slept in because we are still recovering from our embarkation PTSD. Giddy now with the thought of how we are going to spend our twenty-five dollars. I'll probably end up referencing that day for the rest of my life.

Before I forget, I had a banana daiquiri today with John, and it was really good! It's the first one I've ever had, and I loved it. I might get one tomorrow, too. And Kay, the bartender who made the drink, was so sweet. I wasn't going to tell Brad I had one (he was sleeping on a deck chair. See? College student.) because I didn't want him counting drinks, but then at dinner I blurted out that I had a banana daiquiri today and Brad said, "Why is this the first I'm hearing about it?" That's why I love Brad. Because he never disappoints.

The people who work in the Queens Grill dining room are wonderful. And also, strangely, my Dover sole was really good. Like restaurant-good, not cruise ship-good. Which, if you've ever been on a cruise, is high praise indeed. My mom didn't have dessert because she only has it on Sundays (which is tomorrow, and also news to me), but the rest of us did. They made cherries jubilee right behind my dad's chair. I was afraid if they tossed any more rum on those flames, he'd be part of the dessert.

Mostly, we hung around the ship, hopscotching from beverage to beverage and watching old people sleep. After dinner, Brad and I went with Maria and Emily to the Broadway revue in the Royal Court Theatre. I've seen a lot of cruise ship revues in my day; dozens and dozens. And I have to hand it to them, this could be the worst thing I've ever seen in my life. At one point I was so astonished, Brad had to tell me to close my mouth. Now, really, I don't expect a cruise ship revue to be at the level of a Broadway show. But I do expect it to be at the level of a cruise ship show, and, well, let's just say I'm glad they didn't have them come out to entertain us during the boarding clusterfuck of the day before, we were already suffering enough. And why were so many white people singing songs that were not white-people songs? The Latin community does not want to see the version of *West Side Story*'s "America" performed this evening on board the *Queen Mary 2*. And I feel like we could have been canceled just for witnessing the Tina Turner musical medley. But the audience ate it up with a spoon. Which is pretty much how this audience eats everything anyway. If they would have softly whispered, "Just let go," into the microphone we would've lost half the crowd. I mean, they did a tap-dance routine without taps on their shoes. Instead of a raucous dance number, it sounded more like teenagers sneaking in late at night, trying not to wake anyone. (Which, come to think of it, maybe was by design.) It had all the energy of someone peeling a banana.

I feel bad for saying this, because these are struggling young people, but it was *that* bad. (At one point Brad turned to me and said, "Which one do you hate the most?" I knew we'd both pick the same one.) You wouldn't hire a high school kid to make a student film, and then expect us all to sit in a movie theater and watch it, would you? Why do we think it's any different with live performances? The nice thing it did, though, was make us realize how incredible people on Broadway are. We were all forced to watch this because these people wanted to playact being on Broadway. Well, get on Broadway first, and then I'll watch you, how about that? Now I feel terrible for writing all this. But not really. By the time you read this, they'll all be long off the ship and scattered to the winds, anyway. Hopefully not performing anything from the Tina Turner musical ever again.

Tomorrow we're in Halifax, Nova Scotia. I've been there twice before on cruises, and it rained both times. And when I was twenty, I led a teen bike tour through Nova Scotia, and it rained every day, so I don't have high hopes. Oh, wait—I don't hear the piano anymore! And I don't remember when it stopped playing.

July
2

It rained today, but I didn't really care. (All right, I did.) I bet Halifax looks really pretty on a sunny day. Maybe I'll live to see it, but so far that seems pretty unlikely.

Okay, so I'm going to start with the good news. I don't hear the piano playing tonight, so everyone in the Commodore Club has either gone to bed or died. Now the bad news. It's a particularly cloudy night, and in addition to our cabin being directly above the piano bar, it is also, we have just come to discover, directly below the foghorn. Which has been going off every two minutes for the past hour, and will probably continue for the entire night. Looks like I'm going to burn through this bottle of Xanax, which usually lasts me a year, in four days. Two minutes between horn blasts is the exact perfect length of time for you to think maybe it's finally ended, because you haven't heard it in a wh— Oh, wait, there it is again! I'm sure you're reading this, thinking I'm exaggerating. Go download the audiobook now. (I'll make sure they excerpt this part for free.)

Okay, now you're listening to me read this. Hi, thanks for listening to this audio excerpt. What you are about to hear is the exact foghorn sound that is blasting every two minutes in my cabin.

(Play foghorn blast now, please, that I worked on with the sound engineer to get exactly right.)

There. See? I wasn't exaggerating. Every two minutes I clutch my heart. I don't know how many hours this is going to continue, but I'll report back tomorrow. Just know that while I type this, that is happening every two minutes. Also, it makes our cabin vibrate. But there's nothing I can do to make wherever you are vibrate, so you'll just have to take my word for it on that one. Fuck, it just happened again. I wonder if there's someone I can call to trade the foghorn back for the piano. (I just Googled "foghorn location QM2 cabin" and our cabin number was the first thing that came up, so that was not encouraging.) If you gave me a choice between this and someone breaking into our room while I was dead asleep and throwing a freezing-cold bucket of water onto me, I would choose the latter, no question.

I don't know how I can really talk about my day since every blast of the foghorn obliterates a memory, but I'll try. My mom went with Maria and Emily to Peggy's Cove to look at a lighthouse in the fog and eat what Maria said was the best lobster roll she has ever had. I love lobster rolls, and now I really feel like I missed out. Nothing is worse than a bad lobster roll, and nothing is better than a great one. Every human being should be required to have at least one lobster roll a summer. I haven't had mine yet. We will be in Newport on Friday, and I found a place that's supposed to have the best lobster roll in town. I'm hoping my sister will declare the Newport lobster roll the best one she's ever had, so I can stop stressing about missing the Peggy's Cove one.

Brad went with his friend Arlynne (who lives here and came to meet the ship. People live here!) and his mom and John, to explore town and also get lobster rolls, which they didn't like. (Thank God!) I walked with my dad to a local supermarket that had one of those supermarket Starbucks inside it. We had coffees, marveling at how clean Nova Scotia was. I know I can't judge the entire island based on the inside of one supermarket, but I feel like it was a pretty good indicator.

(I'm actually going to recommend that the audiobook version of this essay blasts a foghorn every two minutes while I'm reading it, so you get a sense of what it was like writing it.)

Plus, nothing makes you feel like more of a local than watching people shop for their groceries. To me, a supermarket is the best tourist destination there is. We then walked back to the ship in the rain with our coffees, and Dad and I had lunch by ourselves in the dining room. We each had a glass of rosé. Dad was good company, and definitely in much better shape than the ninety-seven-year-old we pass each meal on the way to our table.

I'm super tired right now (it's almost 1:00 a.m.), but since I know the ship's foghorn is going to keep me awake most of the night, I might as well keep writing. (I think Brad is asleep, although I don't know how that is humanly possible. It's definitely a whole-Xanax, not a half-a-Xanax, kind of night.)

One more thing about today. It's mine and Brad's twenty-second anniversary. (Thank you, Osman, our maître d', for the Baked Alaska tonight. We all loved it. It's Sunday, so my mom could have some. Any dessert you make tableside is for me.)

Brad was a vacation romance (we met in Greece) that has now lasted half his life and a huge chunk of mine. July 2 is my favorite day of the year because no matter what is going on in my life, every July 2, without fail, even if it's only for a brief moment, I am taken back to that day. And what it was like to see Brad's face for the first time as he walked down that winding path in Mykonos and suddenly appeared before me.

(Sound engineer, please insert final foghorn here for effect.)

July
3

Today we were at sea. We mostly hung around, Brad and I still trying to recover from the foghorn assault of the previous night, which lasted until 9:00 a.m. It went on so long, my body is now conditioned to respond with a little spasm every two minutes. Thankfully, today is not foggy. And as I write this, there is neither a horn blasting nor a piano playing. It is quite peaceful. We are in Boston tomorrow, and I'm going to stay on board with my dad while the others explore the city. I love Boston. It's like a miniature New York, but with more annoying accents and shittier restaurants.

I went with my mom to the onboard Starbucks stand-in and had an iced mocha, which I really liked. Having an iced coffee drink at sea seems like the ultimate decadence. Everyone on the ship is strangely nice: all the crew, all the passengers. It's like after the horror of the first night boarding the ship, everyone decided to just chill the fuck out. Maybe it was a blessing in disguise. Literally, if the ship sank, it couldn't be as bad as the embarkation process was.

While waiting for my coffee, I went into one of the shops to buy a teddy bear. (Our twenty-five-dollar credit barely covered two paws and a head.) I still have my teddy bear from the *Queen Elizabeth 2* that I got on board when I was around eight. I always felt ashamed to love teddy bears as much as I did, like it was something that wasn't for little boys, or that I was too old for. It feels so liberating now to just go into a store and buy a teddy bear because I want one. He's sitting on a chair now, facing me as I type this.

Everyone is kind of into the groove of the cruise now. It's almost like I can't remember my life before getting on the ship. After dinner, my parents went to bed, and the rest of us went to the Queens Room to listen to the orchestra's Big Band Night. And let me tell you, they were fantastic. If you want to make an eighty-year-old look thirty, just plop them in front of a big band orchestra. It's basically like putting them in a time machine. The Lindy Hop, the Jitterbug, the Charleston; they knew them all. I think many of the couples on the dance floor took this cruise just to dance. Just to have that feeling once more. How lovely is that?

Suddenly, Maria and I are little kids again, watching the shipboard entertainers as if they were the most famous people on earth. (I guess there was room in that time machine for two more.) The orchestra starts playing Benny Goodman's "Sing, Sing, Sing," and as everyone rushes (well, *their* version of rushes, which is walking slowly) to the dance floor, Brad asks Maria to dance. Brad is a wonderful dancer, and we all watch as he spins my sister around the dance floor, the two of them smiling and laughing as the music continues to build.

I'm going to go to bed now because that's what I'd like to think of as I fall asleep.

July
4

I stay on board the ship with my dad today, while Brad goes with everyone else ashore to explore Boston. (In the rain. What the fuck?) It's just us at our table for eight in the almost-empty dining room (most everyone else has gone ashore as well). My dad tells me about how he first started working for Cunard Line when he was eighteen. He answered an ad in the paper. Something as random as that, and he ended up working there for over forty years, until he retired at sixty-five. But I guess most of life is just as random as that, when you come right down to it.

It's nice to have this time with my dad. It's funny how you always still feel like a kid with your parents, even though he's in his nineties and I'm in my fifties. After lunch we go for a walk and he marvels at the size of the ship. "It's like we're in a movie," he tells me. And I know what he means.

We say hello to people who pass. My father is unfailingly polite. I was worried that this cruise would be too difficult for him, but it has proved to be the opposite. The familiarity of life at sea has eased us into rhythms that go back to my earliest childhood. While we walk, I narrate information about all the public spaces, as if I had built the ship.

An older woman stops us and asks if we know where the cinema is. I tell her we will walk her there so I can show the theater to my father. She is traveling alone. Her name is Betty, and she thanks us for walking with her. "The ship is so large, I'm always getting lost," she tells us. And it is easy to get lost. As we walk with her, my father asks her how old she is. I'm surprised by his bluntness, but Betty doesn't seem to mind.

"How old are you?" she asks him.

"Ninety-two."

"I'm ninety-four," she tells him. I'm completely surprised. I thought she was maybe eighty. Chic and well put together, she seems like someone you'd see at a museum in Manhattan or a Broadway matinee.

"You look great," she tells my dad. "I would've never thought you were ninety-two."

I see my father take this in. He smiles, truly happy, in the way that sometimes only a complete stranger can make you happy. We talk with her a few minutes more, but mostly she talks to my father. She talks to him like she really sees him, and he, in kind, talks to her the same way. It makes me realize how much we ignore people when they get to a certain age. See past them, through them. But watching them talk together, acknowledging each other as only two people with almost two hundred years of combined life between them can, I'm suddenly moved.

We escort Betty to the cinema, where she is going to watch *National Treasure*, already in progress. It doesn't matter what the movie is, though (obviously), or when it started. I think she just comes here to sit for a while each day.

I take my father through the gallery outside the theater that has large black-and-white photos of all the movie stars who have sailed on Cunard. We call out each one we recognize. "Elizabeth Taylor." "David Niven." "Burt Lancaster." It's comforting, I realize, for him to see the faces of so many people from his generation. They are familiar to him, when lately, more and more is not. I walk him back to his cabin, and he kisses me goodbye and thanks me for lunch. Then, before he goes all the way inside, he stops and turns.

"That woman really gave me a lift," he says, smiling. "What was her name?"

"Betty," I say.

"Betty," he repeats, closing the door.

July
5

Where to begin? First off, the foghorn is back. At 3:30 a.m., we both woke up to the blare of the horn. Which then repeated every two minutes, as per its previous schedule. (Again, just a long enough period of time for you to think maybe it's going to stop blasting, and then for it to interrupt that thought with a blast.) It's like some kind of *A Clockwork Orange*–type mind-fuckery. Why would they even put a cabin under the foghorn? To make matters worse, when we woke up this morning, the ship was completely covered in fog, so there's no chance that horn is going to stop anytime soon. It's like the ship is Pigpen and the fog is the cloud of dust that follows us wherever we go. If I have to spend one more day listening to it, I'll lose my mind.

We have been enveloped in a thick blanket of fog since we left Boston. I now look fondly back on the days when I was fixated on the sound of the piano coming from the deck below. Was I ever that young? What I would give for some Nat King Cole or George Gershwin standard to be rising through the floor. So far we have been to two ports, and it has rained in both of them. The rest of the time, we float along the ocean like a ghost ship in mist. Young Gary would have thrown himself overboard by this point, but middle-aged Gary isn't so terribly fussed about the lack of sun on a Fourth of July holiday cruise. (All right, he is.)

To make matters worse, the captain (everyone is still annoyed at him for the horrific boarding process, even though it's not his fault. But who else are we supposed to blame?) comes over the loudspeaker to tell us due to the fog, we might not be able to make our scheduled stop in Newport tomorrow. I haven't been to Newport in thirty years and was super excited to go. I booked us all lunch at the Castle Hill Inn to have lobster rolls. I *really* want a fucking lobster roll, but it's like everything in the universe is conspiring to prevent this from happening.

I know we can't sleep in that cabin another night without going completely mad, so I ask the purser if there's another cabin that we can be moved to, due to the foghorn, and the fact that we're people who like to, you know, sleep. He couldn't be more lovely, and said, "I thought I would be hearing from you two sooner." Which immediately tells me two things: 1. He had us pegged as cunts from the second we boarded, and 2. A lot of people ask to be moved from that cabin.

In any case, the fog becomes a good excuse to engage in the only thing that's more thrilling than changing hotel rooms, and that is changing ship cabins. Whenever I enter a hotel room, I always feel like I'm on an episode of *Let's Make a Deal*. Do I take the first room I'm offered, or do I try for something better? A hotel invariably has people coming in and out every day, so while a better option might not be available on your first or second night, stick it out a little longer, and you may get that corner room, that terrace, that view, or that upgrade. But a ship is a whole other can of worms. Usually, there are very few, if any, options. Short of staying for another cruise, you are often stuck with the cabin you were assigned. And our foghorn cabin was beautiful. Except for, you know, the foghorn. And the piano. (Which, if the foghorn didn't exist, would probably still annoy me.) But the purser tells me there was a couple that had a medical emergency and wasn't able to board the cruise in New York, so there is an available cabin. Yay! What a lucky turn of events! (Well, for us; for them, not so much. I will say this, though: medical emergency or no, I bet it's a hell of a lot sunnier wherever they are.)

The new cabin is at the complete opposite end of the ship, in the aft section. (That's the back, for those of you who have never been on a boat.) Thankfully, the ship is so big, you can't even hear the foghorn back here. (I'm writing from the new cabin now, and it's so quiet I could cry. Until you've been trapped under a foghorn that blasts every two minutes for several days, you never appreciate how wonderful life is *not* hearing a foghorn blast every two minutes. I'm never going to take it for granted again.) I'm so happy writing this now; it's absolute heaven. (Aside from the usual horror of writing.)

I'm still going to take half a Xanax tonight, though, because I don't trust myself to fall asleep on my own, so rattled am I by the previous nights. I'll just wean myself off them when I get back to LA. Or never. Best-case scenario, I live another forty years; what's one Xanax a night until then? (Yeah, I'm taking one, not half.)

Being in a new cabin is suddenly like moving to a new neighborhood. One that's much more convenient to everything you want to go to. It's kind of given me a second wind at this late stage in the trip.

Brad and I host our families in the new cabin before dinner at the ship's alternative restaurant, which is a steak house called the Verandah. When we first boarded the ship, we were told that if we wanted to go to the steak house during the cruise, we would have to book it immediately, as it fills up. My first instinct was to pass, but I booked it for tonight, just to have, figuring we'd probably cancel. But today it's all anyone can talk about. After five days on board, going to a new restaurant for dinner is just the thrill we all need. Brad and I find ourselves talking about it at least a dozen times during the day: "I'm so excited we're going to the Verandah tonight." "What are you having at the Verandah tonight?" "Have you looked at the menu at the Verandah?"

Then the captain comes on the speakers to inform us that due to the fog (it's July!), we won't be able to make our scheduled stop in Newport tomorrow.

Immediately, the talk becomes: "Thank God we're going to the Verandah tonight." "We really needed the Verandah tonight." "Can you imagine if we didn't book the Verandah for tonight?"

This suddenly becomes something important. Something new and exciting to replace what we're losing tomorrow. We go to the restaurant, and they have a beautiful table set for us right by the windows. New waiters, new furniture, new scenery. We are all practically giggling. Picking up the menus, shouting out what we're ordering. It's a fun, long dinner that is pretty much the reason we took this cruise in the first place. To get to spend time together. It really doesn't matter what the weather is (okay, it does), or if we make it to any ports (okay, that matters, too), but the point of the trip was for us all to be together.

My parents didn't meet Brad's mom and her partner, John, until we'd been together ten years. I really can't tell you why; I have no explanation, other than it kind of just didn't happen until then. That's why I love when our families are together. I'm so happy, especially, to see our moms together. I loved Brad's mom from the moment I met her. Debby is a kind, warm, loving person. She's soft-spoken, and has a beautiful smile like her son's, and I've always found her so easy to be around. And I know it makes us both so happy that our mothers get along. My mom pretty much likes everyone, so if she doesn't like you, there's a really good fucking reason. Like if my mom doesn't like someone, they're probably a serial killer or worse.

Tonight I'm sitting across from Debby, and my mom is at the other end of the table. I'm telling Debby how happy I am that we all made the time to take this cruise together. Debby tells me that she feels this cruise has given her an opportunity to get closer to my mom. And I tell Debby how lucky I am to have such a great mother-in-law, and she tells me that she had a terrible mother-in-law who made it very difficult for her. I say, so did my mom! Felicia looks up, having heard that I'm talking about her.

"I'm telling Debby that you had a hard time with your mother-in-law, too."

"Oh, she was awful," my mother says, and means it.

"Mine too!" Debby calls back.

Sitting there watching my mom and Debby bond over a mutual hatred for their mothers-in-law gives me a warm feeling. Yeah, it's for moments like this that I wanted to take this trip.

July
6

It's the last night of the cruise and we're almost back to New York. Considering that we were in Boston two days ago, I could've walked to New York faster. I can see the lights from our new cabin's balcony. (By the way, Brad and I are obsessed with our new room steward, Dong, from the Philippines. From the second we got to the cabin, he has been an absolute delight. If you travel on the *QM2*, please, please, please, ask to be in a cabin that is attended to by Dong. I promise, you'll be thanking me.)

We Are Experiencing a Slight Delay

There's something about the last night of a cruise that is very specific. The second-to-last night is the most festive night of the trip. Everyone drinking, out late, dancing. But the last night, you don't even want to make eye contact with your fellow passengers. The person who was your best friend the previous night is now someone you would cut off your left hand to avoid. We have all mentally checked out at exactly the same moment and just want to get the fuck off the ship at this point. Luggage stacked outside cabin doors, people walking heads down, crew and passengers alike instantly detaching.

There are easily a hundred people on this ship who I'm going to have to dodge on my way off. (Also, never say goodbye to anyone on a cruise. On the last day, you say, "I'll see you in the morning!" The next morning you get off that ship like you're escaping a burning building.)

I'm actually kind of glad we didn't make it to Newport. (Not really. I checked the weather constantly, and it looked beautiful, so I still say we could've made it.) It gave us all the chance to just have a day on the ship (which was moving so slowly, it felt like someone was pedaling it), meeting for coffee, reading on deck (it was sunny! In July! Imagine that!), chatting.

I just wanted to be present for the week. I wanted to spend time with my mom and dad and my sister, Maria, and my niece, Emily, and my mother-in-law, Debby, and her partner,

John, and Brad, who is the best. I said I didn't want to let any tiny, petty things bug me when this started, and to be really honest I don't think I did. (The foghorn was not petty, and I'd like to think I handled it with grace. Mostly.) I've written each entry just before I went to bed each night, and usually finished around 1:00 a.m., while Brad is asleep. I almost stopped this routine three days ago because I wanted to go to bed, but I didn't. I mean, I started it, so I kind of wanted to see how it ended.

Last night we had pictures taken by the ship's photographer for the final Gala Night (their words, not mine). Tonight after dinner, Emily went to get the photos we had purchased earlier in the day. (Emily is the most wonderful travel companion a person could hope to have. She wasn't supposed to even come on this trip; it was supposed to be my brother-in-law, Adam, who I have known since I was sixteen, when Maria first met him at NYU when she was eighteen, and who I think of as my brother. Because he is my brother now. Adam had to go to London for work last-minute, and Emily was his understudy. Normally, I don't like to get the understudy, but in this case, like Sutton Foster [Google it], she stole the show.)

We took several different combinations of photos of the group, and my mom bought Brad and me a few of them. (We went down to the photo gallery to look through them after coffee in the morning. When Maria and I were children, there were walls covered with photos. We would eagerly scan them each day looking for ours, and pointing out ones of other people we knew on the ship, as if they were movie stars in a gossip magazine. Now you just scroll on an iPad.) One of the photos is of all eight of us together, smiling, after the best evening we'd had on the cruise. I also had the photographer take a photo of just me, Maria, Mom, and Dad. Like so many family photos that had been taken by ship's photographers of the four of us for over fifty years. But somehow that's not one of the ones my mother bought for us. She bought it for herself, though, so she'll have it at her house. I hope she puts it in a frame, because I'd like to see it the next time I go home to visit.

Hold on, it's just around midnight. I'm going to step out onto the balcony and see how close the lights of New York are. Be right back.

Oh, wow, we're really close! It'll all be over soon.

chapter nine

I'll Stay in a Hotel, Thanks

I recently talked to a friend who was going to visit relatives in another city and stay in their spare room. Now, if this friend was say, twenty, I would think nothing of it. But this person was over fifty. I would rather never leave my house again for my entire life, to be honest. I have maybe two good hours a day where I'm suitable company. You do not want to see me the other twenty-two. I'm good for at most a dinner.

Now, first off, I understand that not everyone can afford a hotel. But I think that if you've made it to fifty, you should have been able to squirrel away a few bucks to cover a couple of nights at a Radisson.

We Are Experiencing a Slight Delay

I can think of nothing worse than being a guest. (Maybe *having* a guest, but that's it.) I don't want to see you first thing in the morning. I don't even want to see you during the day. And all hosts act as though they only have your utmost comfort in mind, when in fact, each has a hidden set of rules that you will have to decipher as you go. When do they eat, where do they put their dishes, how much time is required to spend with them? It's like cracking the code of a safe.

At least middle-class people have reasonable expectations of their guests. Pitching in with the dishes, helping with the groceries, making your bed—that sort of thing will usually leave you in good stead with your host.

But stay at the house of a rich person, and the expectations are much more insidious and impossible to unravel. Basically, your rich host will insist that you stay with them. They have many extra rooms that just sit empty, they will tell you. If they find out that you are staying at a hotel, they will be offended.

Don't be fooled by this; it is all part of the act. They do *not* want you to accept, and you are expected to know this. The more they insist you stay with them, the more they do not, in fact, want you to stay. If you find yourself falling for this, and you do end up staying with them for a few days (God help you), here's what you should know. As the guest of a rich person, you are now expected to be the perfect companion at all times: entertaining, funny, knowledgeable on all subjects, and with the mind-reading skills of the Amazing Kreskin. You will have to innately discern when to appear and disappear, talk and be silent at the whim of your host's rapidly changing, impossible-to-predict moods. Any tiny infraction you might unknowingly make will be met by your host with the most disproportionate amount of passive-aggressiveness you've ever experienced.

Excuse yourself early one evening, and it's: "Are you okay? You seemed so out of it last night. I was worried." Go to dinner with a friend and the next day it's: "Oh, we get to be graced with your presence tonight! I'm kidding!" (They're not. They're never kidding.)

If a rich person invites you on vacation, this is even worse. You should not think of yourself as a guest, but more of a paid entertainer who has bartered their services for free room and board. And the expected, impossible-to-shop-for thank-you gift for a rich person who has included you in their vacation usually will end up costing the same as a trip to Hawaii. So really, what's the point? Being a dancing monkey for a week is fucking exhausting. And that's what you will be, make no mistake. I guess you just have to weigh how important it is for you to go wherever it is you'd be going, versus basic human dignity.

You should also understand that all rich people think everyone is taking advantage of them. You will inevitably be accused of falling into this category the second your energy flags: "You're so quiet tonight, I feel like I'm on *your* schedule somehow." If you are an alcoholic or a cocaine addict, this will work in your favor, as no one is expected to go to bed before the host, and you'll need all the help you can get to make it through very long nights consisting of subtly and skillfully feeding your host's ego. The cost of being a perfect guest is your sanity. Remember, there are no free lunches. Everything comes with a price. If something seems too good to be true, well, that's because it is. No rich person is a generous host. They are usually bored narcissists looking for a slight diversion in their entitled lives. You are the human equivalent of a new streaming series, nothing more, nothing less. And if you're not amusing enough, they will not watch all episodes. Now, most of us will never be invited to join the wealthy on their yachts or in their villas, but just know that all those people traveling with Mark Zuckerberg or Kim Kardashian or Elon Musk are actually miserable. Really, a night in any Radisson would be preferable, I promise. The daily mental contortions you'll have to go through in the home of any rich person, no matter how beautiful the setting (which you'll stop noticing after the first hour anyway), are not worth it.

When you stay in a hotel, you can do whatever you want, whenever you want. Remember, you always want to be in control while traveling. Come and go as you please. *You* call the shots. Sleep in, get drunk, order room service, who cares?

I'll Stay in a Hotel, Thanks

Nobody really wants to spend all day with you anyway. If one conversation typically has several awkward moments in it, think of all that can go wrong in a day.

I guess it's okay to stay with your sister, or your brother, or your parents. Or your best friend. Someone who can see you in the morning before you've brushed your teeth. Someone whom you can be you with, and not just the version of you that you show everyone else. If you have even a few people like that in your life, you're lucky.

When I was young, I would stay with anyone. On couches, on the floor, wherever. I wanted to travel. I wanted to see the world. I wanted to meet new people. And I did. I met many really wonderful people over the years. Now I'd only stay with three of them—and even they know I'd rather be in a hotel. But maybe I would try it again. Maybe I would want that closeness again. Maybe I can be that person again. I can get so rigid in my thinking as I get older, and that's never a good thing. What's wrong with staying in the spare room? Hanging out in the kitchen, watching TV in your sweats, sharing the ups and downs of an entire day, working through any awkwardness and coming out the other side of it? I could create new memories, a stronger bond, perhaps, with those dearest to me, that would last the rest of my life.

Nah. I don't want to shit in someone else's house.

chapter ten

Packing

For some reason, nobody knows how to do this correctly.
Well, I'm going to teach you. First of all, as I mentioned
earlier, NEVER check a bag. I've traveled for a month without checking a bag, and gone to two weddings and been in
multiple climates. And I probably still brought too much.

You don't need to bring a different outfit for each day
that you're away. Trust me, nobody's going to be clocking what you're wearing every day (all right, maybe I am,
but nobody else.) The trick is, you only ever need to pack
enough clothes for three days. And just plan to do laundry
wherever you go—but never at the hotel, where it costs
twelve dollars to wash a pair of socks that cost two. Find a
local wash-and-fold laundry, and get it all done every few
days for approximately twenty bucks.

Some of my happiest memories while traveling are going

to local laundries. It kind of makes you feel like you live in the city. You have errands to run, stuff to drop off, that sort of thing. I also like local supermarkets and drugstores for the same reason. You can keep the Louvre, thank you, I'd rather spend the afternoon marveling at the dairy aisle in the neighborhood Monoprix. "Look at all the cheese they have!"

Besides, there's nothing like lugging around a giant suitcase to make you look like a dumb tourist. But sweep into the lobby with only a tiny rolly bag and backpack, and suddenly you're the most sophisticated person in the world. Someone who could be breezing in from here or there, jetsetting for months or a weekend, carefree, untouched by the drudgery of daily life. A carry-on bag is a subtle way of letting everyone else know they've done something wrong. Schlepping enough wardrobe changes to film a season's worth of *The Crown* for five days in Aruba.

Three outfits is enough for any trip. Three shirts, three sweaters, three pairs of shoes. One book. Mix, match, and repeat. Traveling becomes so much less stressful when you can pack and unpack in ten minutes. Also, most of the stuff you're bringing is likely not great anyway. Just bring your best stuff—what are you saving it for? And don't wear sweats on the plane, please! (Brad does this, but I do not approve. Knock it off, Brad!) Try to dress a little less like you're on day two of the flu, and a little more like you own clothing that's suitable for something other than working out or sleeping. I assure you, you can also be comfortable sitting for several hours on an airplane in a pair of actual pants with a zipper. (I discussed my feelings on this topic in an earlier essay, but it bears repeating.)

Every time I land in a city and breeze through the baggage claim with my carry-on, I think to myself, *See ya later, suckers!* I'm already checking into my hotel, while these poor slobs are still watching the same bags circle the carousel for the umpteenth time, before they finally realize that theirs is on its way to Amsterdam or Brazil or Denver by now.

Even with only a carry-on, every time I get home, I'll end up realizing I didn't need half this stuff. One suit, one other pair of pants, three shirts, and I'm good to go. You know what? You could actually drop me off with one change of underwear and a toothbrush, and I'd be fine.

Hey, do me a favor. Just one time. Try it out. Take a trip with only a carry-on bag. What's the worst that could happen? You'll feel lighter, freer, unencumbered by so much unnecessary stuff. Pack for only three days. It doesn't matter how many days you're going to be gone for; after three days, just wash and repeat. Also, now you have room to buy something.

After I graduated college, I got a Eurail pass and backpacked through Europe for two months. It's so weird that all the moments I remember most from that trip are the in-between moments. Playing cards in train stations. Showing up at hostels in the middle of the night. Shopping, laundry. All the moments that are supposed to be the nothing moments. The basic, the banal, the boring. The moments between the Coliseum and Pompeii, the Prado and the Parthenon—those are the moments I remember. And you don't need a suitcase for those. You need much less than you'd think. What I usually remember from a trip is a feeling. Was I open to the experience? Was I present? Was I happy?

Brad will tell you that I always forget at least one thing. A swimsuit, a sweater, an appropriate jacket. And he's right. I don't really mind, though. I can pick up a sweater or a swimsuit wherever I am, if I need to. (I mean, if I got Brad on vacation, I can certainly get a swimsuit. More on that in the next essay.)

I just want to be able to pack really quickly. I want to be able to not think about it. I want to travel easy and fast. Because I want to be able to do it again. And again. And again. Quick, light, fleet. Something that you don't make too big a deal out of, where you can throw a few things in a bag and go. (And a book. Remember, always bring a book. Preferably this one.) I'm never more excited than when I zip a bag closed. Ready. (The trip where I met Brad, I planned only a few days beforehand. He remains, to this day, the most expensive thing I've ever brought back from vacation.)

Packing

And if by chance, you ever do see me at an airport and I happen to have a suitcase with me, I ask only that you be kind. After all, every rule has its exceptions. But I promise you this, I will 100 percent get home and say, "I didn't need all this stuff; I should've just brought a carry-on."

chapter eleven

Mykonos

Brad and I are planning a trip to Mykonos. We leave in exactly one week. Based on the previous essay, you already know I'm packing light. Like I can already picture in my head what I'm bringing. I think I'm a visual person (is that a thing?). I can already see what my bag looks like fully packed, so all I have to do is put the stuff in. I'm like Rain Man, but with packing. (Do people still know that reference—"Rain Man"? You know what? I don't care. You guys will either know it, or you'll just blow past it. That's what I do when I don't know something.)

We're also going to the South of France and Paris and London. We're going to be gone one week longer than my perfect amount of time to be away, which is two weeks. Two weeks is heaven. The first week goes by in a deadening crawl, and the second in the snap of your fingers. "I can't believe we've only been gone two days!" is quickly followed by "I can't believe it's almost over!" (Kind of like life. Zero to fifty years is week one, and fifty years to death, week two. I'm, sadly, in week two, the months of my life now being ripped off like calendar pages in a movie montage.)

But three weeks? Three weeks is a different animal. Three weeks might as well be a year. After two weeks of vacation, your sense of time evaporates. That is because no human being is meant to be on vacation for longer than two weeks. And two weeks is a lot, by the way. Rich people are on vacation roughly three hundred days a year. But rest assured, they are bored wherever they are. Once you have nothing left to strive for, it's pretty much dullsville. That's why most billionaire families are filled with, at best, drug addicts and narcissists, and at worst, cannibals. They've got to get their kicks somehow. But for the other 99.9 percent of us, a two-week vacation is enough of a diversion from our normal lives.

Three weeks, though—that's when you start getting texts that read, Are you STILL away? Although, truthfully, I never have any sense of how long a friend is gone for. They could be away five days or six months, and it will feel the same to me. Not unlike how it must be for our dogs while we're away. I mean, it's not like they're checking their phones. They have no fucking clue. I don't even know if a trip is that much different for them than when we go to the grocery store.

Although they *are* pretty bitchy when we return after a few weeks, so they must know *something*.

We're always more aware of what we're doing than what anyone else is up to, anyway. Thinking that everyone's so fascinated with our lives, when no one is really paying that much attention. It always feels like when you're gone a long time, you will have missed so much, when in fact nothing has changed, and nobody is all that aware that you were gone in the first place. So while three weeks will seem like a lot while we're away (especially the third week, where it seems like you can't even remember what your normal life used to be like), in reality, I know from past experience that I will miss nothing, and nobody will give a fuck.

(Except our dogs, who, as just stated, will be super bitchy when we return. Also, they're at home with a friend who stays with them and caters to their every whim, so I don't know what their problem is. If we had actual children, they'd have a shittier life than our dogs.)

Brad and I met on Mykonos while I was there on vacation. As also mentioned in the previous essay, this was a trip that I planned very last-minute. I was thirty-five, and had just shot a television pilot that was still being considered for a series, so I had an unexpected two weeks off while they were deciding. (The show ultimately did not go to series. But on a happier note, the abusive network executive who did not pick it up ended up getting canceled during "Me Too." So that was a nice little cherry on top of that shit sundae.)

I was at Niko's Taverna, having dinner with my friend Sal, when I saw Brad coming down a narrow alley in a sea of people. I don't want to sound too profound or gooey, but something about him immediately drew my eye. (Probably his looks. Okay, definitely his looks. I mean, I just said I was a visual person, so it's not my fault. I will not be superficial-shamed.) But maybe it was something a little more than that, too. Well, probably not when I first saw him. I was literally only attracted to him because of his looks. (Even now, twenty-two years later, the fact that he also has a personality is such a little treat.)

As I saw him coming down the alley, along with hundreds of others, I turned to my friend Sal, indicated Brad, and said, "I want to meet him."

Sal said, "I know the guy he's walking with; we talked on the beach today."

This is what's so great about Mykonos. It's really just a small town. Two days there and you've already seen everyone.

When Brad and Tony reach our table (the other guy's name was Tony; some things you just remember), Sal says hi to Tony, which leaves me free to talk with Brad. The first thing I ask him is his name (I mean, obviously). If he had said Jerry or Alan or Pat, we would not be together today. But Brad. Oh yes. As soon as he said it, I lit up like a Christmas tree. I've always been a sucker for a good name. (I've always wished mine was Miles or Spencer or Grant.)

I offer Brad a bite of my dessert, but he is aloof. At least that's how I remember it. I guess I could go in the other room now and ask Brad his version of events, but that would mean getting up. One of our dogs is sleeping on my lap, and I don't want to disturb him. (So much of my life is spent trying to make two six-pound chihuahuas as comfortable as possible.)

In any case, Brad's a bit standoffish. For all of five minutes. He tells me he's a model (he's not), and he's in Athens doing catalog work (he's not, and anyway, who goes to Athens to model?), and came to Mykonos last-minute for the weekend. (To think that had this now-canceled network executive not been torturing me for months over this pilot, we would have never met.) When he tells me he's twenty-three, I lie and tell him I'm thirty-two. In my defense, it's not that much of a lie, and at the time I didn't think he'd be coming home with me forever, for Christ's sake. (Also, he's only twenty-three for another few weeks, thank God, so we're eleven years apart, not twelve. I round it down to ten anyway. I find out, in short order, that his previous boyfriend was actually ten years older than me, so *he* was the one who was robbing the cradle.)

Brad stands there talking to me, now sharing my dessert, all his defenses down after the first bite. The aloof shield immediately lifted. I can see him trying on this personality affectation, but it clearly does not fit. I mean, he's Canadian. They don't have more than five minutes of aloofness in them.

Oh, wait, Brad just came into my office as I'm writing this. Hold on, let me ask him what he was like when we first met.

Brad says he was not aloof, that he was sweaty (he was). He adds, "I wasn't trying to be aloof, I was trying to play it cool because you were so hot." (These are his exact words, people, not mine!)

"Did I tell you I was thirty-two?" I ask.

He corrects me. "You told me you were thirty-three, but you were thirty-five." And he corroborates that I definitely offered my dessert. He's saying he didn't think he had any. "It doesn't seem very me, to be eating a stranger's dessert," he says.

"Yet you were making out with me on the dance floor thirty minutes later," I point out.

"That *does* seem very me."

We spend the night at my hotel (which I had just moved to, abandoning my previous hotel because it was too far from town), and in the morning he goes back to where he's staying. Wait a second—Brad left my office. Let me call him in here again, because this part is fuzzy.

"Brad, when you left my hotel that first morning, where did you go?"

"Back to my hotel," he answers.

"Was it a hostel?" I ask. "I feel like it was a hostel."

"It wasn't a hostel. It was seven drachmas a night," he says.

"That seems impossibly cheap."

"I remember it being seven. I split it with Tony, so it was fourteen, I guess."

I'm not sure if I can trust Brad on the price, but I will say that it was as cheap a room as you could possibly find on the island.

"Did I ask you to bring your stuff with you and stay with me at my hotel, after that first night?"

"Yes," he says with certainty.

"I remember you had a big suitcase. Why did you have so much stuff with you, if you were just initially going to stay for the weekend?"

"Because I wanted to bring all my nice stuff with me."

"I don't remember any nice stuff."

"I had Miu Miu boots, I had a Versace shirt, I had a bunch of stuff. I don't know why I had boots with me."

"But there was a lot of terrible stuff, too," I say.

"Well, at the time I didn't think it was terrible, but yes."

"Did you think it was weird that I asked you to stay with me after one night?"

"No, because I was like a free spirit, it never even crossed my mind."

"Plus, we were both a little slutty."

"Yeah."

"I remember never being apart as soon as you returned with that huge suitcase."

"Oh yeah, no, we were never apart."

"When exactly did you sing 'I Dreamed a Dream' from *Les Miz* as Patti LuPone to me?"

"I think it was on the second night, as we were watching the sunset in Little Venice."

"I think so, too. Even though I never told you, I think that's when I fell in love with you."

"Aww." (At this point, he *should* say, *That's when I fell in love with you, too*, but he doesn't.)

"When did you fall in love with me?" I ask. "Do you know?"

"I think it was in Santorini." (We went to Santorini after Mykonos for two days.)

"So this means I might have fallen in love first?"

"Potentially, yes," Brad says, "but you're a little more lesbian than I am."

So I guess we both fell in love during that first trip, within a week of each other. I can live with that.

"What do you remember most about that week?" I ask him.

"You."

I like the way he answers this. Without even thinking. How can it still make me feel so good all these years later?

"What else?"

"Tearing into the seafood platter together in Santorini, and crying when you left in Athens."

"I remember all the giant bottles of toiletries you had with you."

"I had *one*. Aloe vera gel. Which I ended up needing, because I was sunburnt."

"I remember huge shampoo bottles."

"What was it? Like Herbal Essence?"

"Uh-huh, and I made you throw them out."

"Shocker. I remember you were wearing Helmut Lang underwear."

"I don't ever remember owning a pair of Helmut Lang underwear."

"I also remember Pierro's," he says. Pierro's was the club that everyone went to, which sadly is no longer there.

"What do you remember about Pierro's?"

"The drag queen on the balcony who would scream, 'Showtime!' And I remember dancing to 'Your Disco Needs You.'"

"I remember that, too. That was fun. Are things less fun now?"

"Yes. Definitely."

"Is there anything else from that first week you can think of that really stands out for you?"

LONG PAUSE. STILL WAITING. Then: "Feeling like I'd met the person I was going to be with for the rest of my life."

"Did you really feel that?"

"Yeah. Why do you think I came all the way to LA?"

"I thought it was a summer romance, but secretly I think I thought the same thing."

Brad's about to feed the dogs now. I call out another question.

"How many times do you think we've been to Mykonos?"

"Ten? Don't you think?"

"Yeah, at least ten. Are you excited to go next week?" I ask.

"Yeah. Oh, the other thing I remember are the sunsets!"

"*Is* the sunsets."

I'm not sure how many times exactly we've been to Mykonos, but a lot. After this summer, we might take a break for a while. What's funny is that for twenty-two years, we've always stayed at the same hotel. The one where we spent our first night. I call to him in the next room, one more time.

"Have we ever stayed anywhere other than the Belvedere?"

"Uhhhhh . . . no."

"We talked about it a lot, though. Right?"

"Yeah, up until this year, when you took that woman on a wild-goose chase."

"It wasn't a wild-goose chase; it was just thorough research of a new hotel," I say. (Maybe it was.)

The truth is, we have talked about staying on another part of the island, or at a different hotel, or renting a house, every single time we've gone back. And for some reason, every single time, I can't bring myself to stay anywhere else. But maybe after this trip, it will be different. I'm just terrified of actually staying somewhere else, and then thinking we should've stayed at the Belvedere the second we check in. This is not an unlikely scenario.

It's not as if every time we go to Mykonos, I'm trying to re-create that first trip. Although that kind of did happen at the beginning. Everything was too "special," though. It all was a bit too precious and weighted, and the pressure to re-create something that is impossible to re-create made everything else fall short somehow. But then we took a break for maybe seven years or so. And when we returned, we were just focused on the present. Not worrying about going to all our "spots," or making every moment meaningful: "This is where this happened; this is where that happened." We just behaved normally and hung out.

But the one thing I could never change was the hotel. Even up until two weeks ago, we were going to stay somewhere else. Maybe we should have. Maybe that's the last thing that has to go; the last thing I'm holding on to for some reason. I don't know. I'll let you know when we're back.

The first time I was in Mykonos, after I had just graduated from college, I don't even think I went out dancing or to the bars. Isn't that odd? I must have, but for some reason, I don't remember it. I didn't pick anybody up, I didn't kiss a boy, I didn't fall in love. I didn't a lot of things, that first trip. I did go back a year later, though, but again I don't remember much of the trip.

It wasn't until I went again when I was thirty-five, that I remember everything. I went with the same friend from college, Sal, that I had gone with thirteen years previously on that very first trip. And maybe in a bid to make up for lost time, I was a complete whore. Packing everything into those two days before I met Brad, that I didn't on my previous trips. And then when I met him, well, it was just so easy. Like he had always been there.

When the trip ended and we said goodbye, we could not text. I could not scroll through photos on my phone. I had to go home and get my film developed at Rite Aid like an animal. And there, back in LA, shuffling through the pictures of that week, I knew. I emailed him. (We *could* do that, thank God. People checked their email, at the time, with roughly the same frequency as a haircut.) And I arranged for him to visit a few days later.

I made no promises, except to take it one day at a time

Mykonos

(no, I'm not in AA)—and now here we are, twenty-two years later. Sometimes I think I went there looking for him. But no, it was probably just random as fuck. When we return to Mykonos, though, and we talk about that first week, sometimes it's almost like we're talking about two other people. A story that has been passed down to us by some other couple. We are recounting their story, not ours. And then, other times, it's like we're still on that same first trip. Like our whole lives together have existed only on this island.

We've been going there long enough to see it change. Change so much that last year, we decided to take a break. To not go again for a while (ever?). A certain charm, a certain freedom, a certain spirit is missing. Replaced by the same things that replace everything everywhere that was once charming, special, gay. One hundred euros for a sun bed, where previously a towel would do. There are other places in the world that inevitably replace those original charming spots. But I didn't meet Brad at any of those other places. I haven't been returning thirty-five years to anywhere else.

I will let this trip be what it wants to be. I don't mind that I am not looked at in the same way (in any way) in the bars and clubs. I don't mind that I am not twenty-two or thirty-five. Until I do, I guess. And then I don't again. That's how it goes, I suppose, when one is no longer twenty-two or thirty-five.

Anyway, I am off. Again. I'll report back what the trip
was like when I return. I'll leave a big chunk of empty page
just after this to delineate the time passage. So funny to
think it will only take you seconds to get from the before
part to the after, but for me there will be weeks between
them that could contain anything. And I don't want them to
go by in the blink it will take you to get from this sentence
to the next.

I'm back. Fuck. Well, it took me a lot longer to get from
the previous sentence to this one than it did you, that's
for sure. I suppose I should read what I've already written
before I jump back in again. I'm also wondering if it was always in the back of my mind that when I returned, I would
continue this essay, and it would seem like not only did the
trip go by in a blink for you, the reader, but also for me, the
writer. I was aware that it would probably seem that way
to me, too, once I had planted that seed in my head before
I left. That the three weeks would dissolve as quickly as a
sugar cube dropped into a cup of hot tea (I was also in Lon-

don). So here I am, after three weeks of thinking, as soon as I type "I'm back," it will be like I never left in the first place. Like why bother going anywhere, when you get right down to it? Everything evaporates in a moment. I guess I know why . . . but still. It seems like a lot of effort for something that left no tangible mark except a fading tan. (All right, I'm going to go back and read what I wrote before I left now. Okay, done.)

But here's the other thing. The trip may have shifted my thinking—definitely about what I was writing before I left. First off, I was correct about returning to the Belvedere Hotel. Initially, it takes me a full thirty-six hours to get over thinking I've made a terrible mistake. That there is somewhere else I should be. Better. Newer. Nicer. And having *that* trip instead. Then, suddenly, it shifts. There's no other place I want to be. I like it here. Where I am. There's something to be said for liking where you are.

Some hotels have a soul, and this one definitely does. Whether it's because of our history there, or because of the hotel itself, I can't say. Does it even matter? Some of the people have worked there as long as we've been going. It's kind of like our house while we're there. I expected to go this time and, when we left, to have the feeling that we would not return for a while. That we had done it. That it was time to move on. But weirdly, the opposite happened. I said I was going to let the trip be what it was going to be, and I did. (I feel like I have to remind myself of this often. Let things be what they want to be, instead of trying to impose onto them what I think they should be.)

Sometimes reminding myself helps. Giving up control is never easy for me. I'm sure it's a defense mechanism that I adopted early on to protect myself from getting beat up in school. But it has come in handy; I can plan a good trip. (The trick is, after you plan it, to just let go. And that can take a minute.)

And yes, being gone for three weeks is too long. I can say now with complete authority the perfect amount of time to be away is seventeen days. Two weeks of solid vacation, allowing for a day of travel each way, and one day to acclimate. Anything more, and it's basically too much candy on Halloween. There's a limit to everything. Even pleasure. Also, it's hard to maintain enthusiasm for twenty-one days. There's just so much time you can spend staring at a view. I mean how long is one supposed to look at the Eiffel Tower for? It's not like it does anything.

(A place has a way of pushing you out when it's time to leave. A favorite restaurant you return to for your final night is suddenly limp and uneventful; a last drink with a friend, more perfunctory than celebratory. Everything conspiring to push you toward home. An entire country telling you, *Okay, you've had enough.*)

But Mykonos. I don't know why I keep going back. I mean,

it gave me Brad—I owe it. After all these years, Brad and I know how to do this island right. What beaches to go to, where to eat, when to get up, when to go to sleep. We fall into the rhythms again so easily. "Why are we back?" dissolves seamlessly into "I'm so happy we're back."

There are moments, inevitably, where my mind tricks me, and this familiar person I'm with, this familiar island I'm on, these familiar roads, restaurants, people, make me think I am thirty-five again. That I look like everybody else around me, and not the elder statesman I have become. And all it takes is a quick glance in a shop window to snap me out of it, but the sensation returns again and again. I can't determine, like so many things, if it's delightful or depressing.

I won't tell you who we meet on this trip, who we talk to, where we go. I won't bore you with all that. Usually, the most wonderful moments are completely banal in the retelling. And I won't tell you about France and London, because this essay is about Mykonos. But I will tell you about something that happens on our last day on the island.

I take our laundry into town to the local wash-and-fold. (Taking my laundry to the local wash-and-fold is perhaps the most therapeutic thing I do while traveling. I never feel more at home in a place than I do while walking down a neighborhood street with a bag of dirty clothes. The laundromat is located right across from the bus station. This isn't the kind of bus station that you are imagining. This is merely a small parking area where two or three buses navigate the incredibly tiny streets that take travelers from the carless center of town to the outlying ports, where they will then take small boats to the various beaches. This is usually the preferred method of transportation for backpackers and student travelers—those who are not renting cars, or staying in expensive hotels with their own shuttles, or taking taxis.

These are the same buses I took thirty-five years ago on my first visit to the island, long before even Brad. I was twenty-one, and I packed onto those buses with everyone else and rode them to places named Platis Gialos and Psarrou, and got on small boats that took us to Paradise Beach and Super Paradise, and farther out, Elia. And you would get off these small boats, directly into the water, and trudge through it onto shore. And you would take your towel and find a spot to lay it down. You'd go into the water to swim, read a book, talk to whoever was nearby.

And late in the afternoon or early in the evening, you would wait for the little boats to return you once again to places named Platis Gialos and Psarrou, and get on the buses that were waiting to take you back. To this very spot. Where I now sit on a bench with my bag of laundry. Watching the young people climb on board. Watching until it pulls away.

chapter twelve

Noma

Noma is a restaurant in Copenhagen famous for being impossible to get into. Also, I suppose, for its food and many, many courses. Let's just say, this is not the type of place where one asks for dressing on the side. Or anything really. You get what they give you. And you like it. This typically would be my worst nightmare, yet I was desperate to go.

But when it came time to booking a trip to Copenhagen, I always changed horses midstream—preferring instead Spain or Italy, or someplace else in Europe where the chance of rain on any given day did not hover around 90 percent. Now, I'm a good sport if it rains for one day (two days, TOPS), lying the way every other traveler lies about how we're actually happy it's raining, how beautiful the city looks like this, how fun it is to stay inside, sleep in late, get lost in a museum, that shit. But really, I'm miserable.

We Are Experiencing a Slight Delay

If I'm getting on a plane for twelve hours, I'd like to get off someplace where the sun hits you like a punch in the face. There's nothing worse than arriving in a new city during a downpour, everyone bundled against the elements as they fight their way to a taxi or bus. No, thank you. I want to walk out of an airport and feel as though I've stepped into a pizza oven.

The stress of booking a trip to Copenhagen and then dealing with the extreme probability of rain every day is almost too much to bear. As I'm writing this, I check the weather there now, and it says possible rain the next eight out of ten days. I know if you go in the summer the weather is better, but the sun is also out for twenty hours a day then, and that just feels like overkill to me. You can't make up for 335 shitty days with one month of straight sunlight. How does that not drive a person insane?

I also feel like it's a city you can cover in twelve hours. The kind of place that seems sprawling when you first get there, but after thirty minutes of walking, you find yourself back where you started. Knowing the streets like a local by dinnertime.

I suspect, too, that it's the kind of place I will love. Bleached wood floors. Lots of benches and architectural light fixtures. Baristas being elevated to the status of pop stars. And yet here I am in Rome or Madrid again, with a plate of pasta or paella, sweating at 10:00 p.m.—which to me seems infinitely preferable to wearing a rain slicker in July. I guess I need to be someplace warm that's within an hour's flight from Copenhagen, so I can monitor the weather from there and be ready to hop on a plane at a moment's notice. But then I don't know how I would get a reservation at Noma, which usually has to be booked as far out as one would reserve a wedding venue. Like, really, who knows what they're going to be doing sixteen months from now?

Also, and this plays a big factor, years ago, while I was working in London for several months, I went to Stockholm for a long weekend in December, and it was sunny every day. The sunlight only lasted for like three hours each day, but it was perfect. Every person I came in contact with said this was the most perfect weather they had ever seen in Stockholm in December. Which only means odds were strong that when I returned to Scandinavia, I was in for a total shit show.

There was no way I'd get to repeat that experience; that's not how life works. Copenhagen was ready and waiting to piss down rain on me, whenever I decided to go. There really was nothing to be done, except to avoid Denmark altogether for as long as I could. Plus, if I booked a trip to Copenhagen just because I had a dinner reservation at Noma, then I would be obsessed with tracking the weather there each day until our trip began, and I just didn't have that kind of time. On top of that, the likelihood of me actually being able to eat, much less enjoy, any food at this restaurant seemed almost nonexistent. A place where duck brain and reindeer penis appear on the menu in slots more typically reserved for roast chicken and spaghetti.

But as luck would have it, Brad and I are invited to a pop-up of Noma in Mexico while they are renovating their Copenhagen location. We don't even have to make a reservation. This was several years ago, and to be honest, I'm not even sure now why we were invited. Something to do with something nonsensical, no doubt. (Isn't everything?) The night of the dinner, though, still burns bright in my memory. (Unlike the sun in Copenhagen.)

I believe the meal is to be twenty courses. I usually ask for the check at the same time I order dessert, so that lets you know where my head is at from the get-go. There's nothing I hate more than a tasting menu. It's like being taken hostage, but by a restaurant. The bill usually as expensive as a ransom. (I'm sure there are people that have been kidnapped and returned for less money than a meal at Noma.)

But I am willing to try anything once (not really, but in this case, sure), and who wouldn't want a chance to experience what is considered the best restaurant in the world? (I don't know how one comes to this conclusion—do they actually try every restaurant in the world? You know what? I'll leave that for another essay.) Besides, I love Mexican food, and this pop-up Noma (also, on a side note, enough with the pop-ups) is to feature the cuisine of Mexico, and offer only local ingredients. As far as I know, there are no reindeer roaming the streets of Mexico, so at least I'm off the hook on that front.

Really, what's worse than people standing over you while you're tasting food you didn't even order, awaiting your verdict? Not much. So I'm not sure why I'm so excited about finally going to Noma. I guess it's the whole ethos of the place that really captures my imagination. A restaurant that you have to study up on before you go. You can't just show up there like you're going to any fucking trattoria or bistro. No, this is restaurant as theater. As church, even. And you are not a guest, rather an acolyte. The lucky few, the chosen. For what, it remains to be seen.

First off, I should say that the restaurant, in a clearing beside a beach in Tulum, is beautiful. The impermanence of it is perhaps its most extraordinary feature. Constructed out of local materials only for these several months, it appears among the foliage like a mirage.

The weather is perfect. (Yaaaaaas, Mexico.) Brad and I are both very excited, but Brad, being the more adventurous eater, is wary for me.

"Are you sure you want to do this?" he asks, as if we are about to dive off a waterfall or go kitesurfing. (Which, for me, this kind of is.)

I assure him I'm fine. I feel the need to experience a

dinner the length of Wagner's Ring Cycle at least once in my life.

We go through several layers of greeters before we arrive at our table. I've gone to weddings and talked to fewer people, and we haven't even sat down yet. There is not a noun uttered that isn't followed by a monologue. "Your chair is made from zapote wood discovered along the Yucatan Peninsula by one of our waitstaff, Mikkel, while surfing with his twin daughters, Malthe and Bodil. You'll meet them all shortly." My smile muscles already ache as I snap the napkin onto my lap.

Brad and I exchange a look that simultaneously communicates, *Oh, shit*, and *Let's just go with it*.

Let me state for the record that going to dinner at Noma is not like going to dinner at, say, a restaurant. That is, if your experience of going to restaurants thus far, like mine, consists of eating food and having a conversation that is occasionally interrupted by your server bringing something to the table. Nothing resembling that will happen during your time at Noma. Here, you are almost incidental to the experience. This is the ultimate in dinner theater.

Each course arrives with a description that could be performed as an audition piece for the School of Drama at Yale. Like Shakespeare, they could be revisited again and again for decades to come, future generations discovering more and more within the meaty text. The introduction to our cutlery alone could rival Mercutio's Queen Mab speech.

Now, I'm not saying we aren't enjoying ourselves, or don't truly marvel at all the care and attention that has gone into everything. The perfect open kitchen, where a dozen remarkably similar-looking people move in sync to music only they can hear. An endless supply of smiling young people dressed in soothing cotton earth tones. How could you not be hanging on their every word? I guess it's just hard to maintain that level of enthusiasm for such an ungodly number of courses. Most of the dishes are made from items that I didn't even know were edible. "Cold Masa Broth with Lime and All the Flowers of the Moment" was the name of our fourth course. By this time, they could have taken the woman's purse sitting next to us, dumped its contents out over a frying pan, served us a fried lipstick, and I wouldn't bat an eye.

A few hours in, and I'm afraid to ask where the bathroom is because by the time they tell me how it was built I'll have already shit myself. The dinner has now gone on longer than the flight we took to get here.

Brad is impressed with how well I'm doing. The truth is, I'm so exhausted from smiling and listening attentively that it's easier to eat whatever's on my plate, than to have to explain why I don't like it. Not liking something does not seem to be an option here. There is no room for any facial expression other than complete awe.

What could best be described as the entrée arrives. We are told that it is the specialty of the Noma Tulum experience. "Tostadas with Ant Larvae," if I'm not mistaken, is what the dish is called. It looks like a spoonful of corn topped with some pepper on a cracker. Now, normally, I'm not one for ant larvae (to be fair, they are calling it *escamoles*, which I admit does sound a lot more appetizing than "ant larvae"), but since they appear to be as tiny as a speck of pepper, I'm not all that fussed.

Brad can't believe I ate it.

"Why not?" I say. "It's so small, you can barely even taste anything."

Dessert follows in short order. It is something that's not supposed to be turned into ice cream that has been turned into ice cream.

After dinner, we are invited to have drinks with the staff in a super-chic lounge area that they have built out of a fallen palm tree and some coconuts. At this point in the evening, I already know more about the waitstaff than most of my immediate family members, so we politely decline. It's not like we didn't have a great time. Everyone was wonderful, and the food was gorgeous. We could sense the love and care that went into everything. It's just that, I guess, after a while, I can't take in any more new information, and

I turn off. Having to keep a look of amazement on one's face for five hours straight can be stressful (also probably not very good for your face). I mean, they take this shit seriously. I'm not saying it seemed like a cult, but I'm not saying it *didn't* seem like a cult, either. I mean, everyone was dressed the same, looked the same, and sounded kind of the same, so there was that, you know, culty thing. But it was also fabulous. Once. Most experiences shouldn't be repeated anyway. I was happy that I got to go.

(Sometimes it's hard to tell if something is delicious, if you have never tasted anything like it before. Like was it delicious or weird? I went with delicious in the moment, but weird the next day when I shamefully confessed to Brad that maybe it was all just meh. Like I would have preferred a hamburger. He agreed instantly, which is why we've been together twenty-three years.)

Months after we return from Tulum, Brad and I are at my parents' house having dinner with my family, and he tells everyone how I ate ant larvae in Mexico. Nobody can believe it. I mean, I didn't even eat a shrimp until I was forty. I tell them that it was no big deal, though. That it looked like tiny specks of pepper.

Brad says, "What are you talking about?"

I say, "It looked like pepper, it was kind of a scam. Just little black dots on corn; there was nothing to it."

He tells me that there was no corn. That *that* was the ant

larvae. I tell him he must be mistaken, as it looked exactly like corn. He then Googles "ant larvae" and shows me the image on his phone.

It does indeed look like corn. If it's possible to get retroactively sick, I manage to do it. My stomach still flips at the thought of it.

Recently, it was announced that Noma in Copenhagen would be closing, and it made me sad. Maybe I'll get there before they serve their last meal. Maybe I'll get one of their last reservations. Because I kind of want to go now more than ever. I'm checking the weather on my phone as I type this. It doesn't look bad!

chapter thirteen

A Thing That Annoys Me While Traveling

This is something that annoys me while traveling. Even more so than your flight being delayed once you're already on the plane, and the pilot not informing you what's going on. You used to be able to complain to your flight attendant in moments like these. Ask, "Hey, are we going to be taking off, or not?" No more. People have been thrown off planes for less. The tables have turned, and flight attendants now have as much power as Kim Jong Un. Wielding it as indiscriminately, too.

And you know what? Good for them. Believe me, if I were a flight attendant I'd be having passengers dragged off the plane for their outfits alone. (Sometimes, though, weirdly, you'll get on a flight where all the passengers seem to be in sync. Everyone is quiet and respectful and patient, and you get off the plane thinking, *I like people*. Only to be reminded on your next flight how much you loathe and despise them.) Once you are on a plane, you are their prisoner. You have no recourse, other than smiling and being grateful for every little tidbit of information thrown your way.

But even more annoying than that is the passenger sitting next to you striking up a conversation. I don't know why it is that people feel the need to tell their life story to whomever chance has happened to toss into the seat next to them. No one wants to hear it, I assure you. Certainly not me. And yet I can't tell you how many times I have been seated behind two strangers who strike up a conversation that doesn't end until baggage claim. Talking like two long-lost siblings. (Okay, I guess some lunatics *do* want to hear a stranger's life story, if only so they can tell theirs.)

One of these people, no doubt, will have a job in marketing or sales, about which all of us within earshot will learn every last detail over the next excruciating hours, their seatmate hanging on to their every word as if it were Winston Churchill delivering a wartime speech.

These are the same people that speak in a volume usually more suited to stadiums. The same people who are completely unaware that it is possible to modulate the volume of one's voice to a level that is appropriate to their surroundings. No, these people speak in the same volume they would at a wrestling match or heavy metal concert. They want you to hear every last boring detail of their dull, never-ending story in Dolby Stereo.

I always think, *Put the chatty person next to me—I'll shut them up! Don't seat two of them next to each other!* I can shoot my seatmate down within the first five seconds of seeing them. Saying "good morning" in a way that lets them know these are the only words we will be exchanging this flight. It's a deft performance, if I do say so myself. I don't think even Meryl Streep could accomplish what I can in two words. I've been honing that performance for decades. If they don't feel a shiver down their spine after that, well, I'd be surprised. My dead-eyed, uninflected greeting followed by the ceremonial insertion of my ear pods really drives the message home.

I don't know what most of my friends actually do for a living; I certainly don't want to know what this random person sitting next to me does. Nor do I want to hear about, God forbid, their children. Or where they are from, or why they are going to where they are going. I don't care; I'm barely interested in my own life.

For the duration of the flight, I communicate with only

slight facial expressions. A tiny smile means, *Would you mind getting up so I can pass by to use the bathroom, please?* A small nod upon return is *Thank you*. Too big a smile or nod might incite conversation. You must regulate this to perfection. You are a wall. Immovable. Your relationship to this person is based solely on bathroom access.

The only thing worse than sitting behind two strangers getting to know each other is sitting behind two strangers getting to know each other over drinks. The drudgery of an ordinary flight elevated by these two bozos to the celebratory status of New Year's Eve. The drunker they get, the louder they talk. The words "spreadsheets" and "fourth quarterly" worm their way through my earplugs as I try to sleep on a pillow the size and consistency of a kitchen sponge.

It's gotten to the point that when I am flying alone, or Brad is, we instantly text once on board to let the other know how things are shaping up. It's 6:00 a.m., and the guy in front of me is talking about meeting his sales quota is a typical text I'll receive from Brad once he's in his seat. My job is to talk him down. Maybe they'll go to sleep or watch a movie, I'll text back, while knowing the odds of this are not great. The text you always want to send or receive is My situation looks good. It doesn't always hold up until landing, but it's usually a positive indicator at the start of a flight. The person next to me, the people around me, all seem to appear to be on the same page; no one chatting, people preparing little nests to sleep in . . . well, there's no happier feeling, is there?

Years ago, while flying alone to New York, I am seated next to someone who I instantly recognize. It is Judy Collins, the folk singer quite popular in the '60s and '70s, most famous for "Both Sides Now" and her rendition of "Send in the Clowns." When I was a child, in my basement in Queens, I listened to "Both Sides Now" endlessly. It's a melancholy song about heartbreak (written by Joni Mitchell and later recorded by her as well, but Judy's version came first, so don't come for me), and something about it really hit home for ten-year-old Gary. I had not thought of this song in many years. Or of me listening to it and singing along in my basement. Had not thought of Judy Collins in many years. Not until this moment, when she is suddenly seated next to me.

I smile and say good morning, friendlier than usual to be certain, but I do not betray any recognition. She smiles back. She sits by the window and does not get up for the entire flight. There is no opportunity for me to stand for her, smile, be gallant. I watch a movie, I sleep, I read. At a certain point in any flight, it becomes too late to exchange even the simplest of pleasantries. We have both signed this contract of silence.

The flight ends, and I get up and smile and nod. She

smiles back. Not even an overhead bag that I can help take down for her. Listening to her sing "Both Sides Now" over and over again in my basement, lying on the carpet. It was like she was singing it for only me. Maybe I should say thank you. Maybe I should break my rule. But she is already gone.

chapter fourteen

A Travel Tip

I'm going to share with you a little tip, something I used to do when I was traveling on the cheap, but wanted to stay somewhere fabulous. As an example, I'm going to use a trip I took to Hawaii while I was working as a bellman at the Paramount Hotel in New York City. I was dating someone at the time (all right, I might have been living with them. Who remembers? Everything is a blur before Brad), and we decided to go to Hawaii. (This person will now disappear from the essay.)

I was not good at making money then, but I was good at spending it. My entire livelihood depended on the largesse of strangers. (Once, I got a two-hundred-dollar tip, and everything I spent for the next few weeks, I attributed to that found money. Dinners, clothes, an airline ticket, you name it. That tip probably ended up costing me several thousand dollars.) I did not have a ton of extra money lying around. (Actually, I was in debt—I had *zero* extra money.) And what little I had saved I used on traveling. (I had saved nothing, each trip sinking me a little farther into debt.)

Like all gay men, I wanted to stay in hotels I couldn't afford. Places I had seen only in the glossy pages of a magazine. (I miss magazines. I know they still exist, but not really.) *Condé Nast Traveler* was my bible, and I mentally planned each trip as if I were a Rockefeller or Getty. Hotel du Cap, Cipriani, Claridge's—I was going to stay at all of them. In my mind, at least. But I did eventually come up with a little work-around while traveling without, well, money.

First off, locate someplace cheap but not disgusting. I found it best to not book anything until I arrived at my destination. I know this seems scary to most of you, but believe me, it can work to your advantage.

On this particular trip to Hawaii (with aforementioned unnamed person that I was kind of living with), I stayed in a type of bed-and-breakfast place. And by "type of" bed-and-breakfast place, I mean a bed-and-breakfast. Typically, I would avoid a bed-and-breakfast like the plague. (Even then, when I had nothing but debt and a dream, I was repulsed. Eating breakfast with strangers is perhaps the worst travel concept ever conceived.) But this one was charming, with beautiful grounds and ocean views, for a fraction of what you'd pay for at an actual hotel. I had read about it in a guide book (pre-internet, I used to research travel like Woodward and Bernstein poring over the Watergate papers).

I went in person to see it, not booking it in advance, to make sure it lived up to its description. (You couldn't look at photos online then; you had to picture things, like, in your head.) Yes, I risked its being fully booked, but things weren't really fully booked before Instagram existed. You could always wrangle up something, and with the front desk clerk standing in front of you, the prices were usually a bit more flexible. I would usually ask to see every room available, and then ask for the cheapest one. And then ask to be upgraded from that one. I mean, the room *was* empty; they'd just shown it to me. Also, if you ask nicely, you'd be surprised what people will give you. And if you happen to be young, your chances are exponentially much higher. Try it. And this isn't even the travel tip.

Okay, so here's the tip: Let's say you're away for one week. For six of those nights, you will stay in cheap lodgings. But for the one other night, you will stay at—in keeping with the example of my trip to Hawaii with you-know-who—the Four Seasons. Again, you book the cheapest room. But you arrive at 9:00 a.m. Your room will not be ready, but not to worry, you will store your bags and have use of all the hotel's facilities for the day. Then, the following morning, at what should be your included breakfast (Make sure it's included! You can always get free breakfast out of them!), you treat it as though it's brunch, loading your plate with enough to get you through the day. Any kind of food or beverage costs a fortune at these five-star hotels, but they usually offer enough free amenities for you to gorge yourself without having to actually spend any money.

The next day, you do not check out at noon. (I always ask for a 2:00 p.m. checkout wherever I am, and then leave at three. Just tell the front desk you'll be down in a minute when they call. It works, trust me. And if they say they can't give you a 2:00 p.m. but they can give you 1:00, say thank you, and then still come down at 3:00.)

Then, after you check out, you store your bags again and use the pool, the beach, and all the hotel has to offer for the rest of the day. Often these places have free sunset drinks and snacks. Make sure to stay for those. If handled correctly, this could be your dinner. So essentially for the cost of one night, you will get two full days. I usually saved this treat for the end of the trip because once you've stayed at a Four Seasons in Hawaii, you won't want to go back to your now-shitty bed-and-breakfast. (And, for any young person traveling today, these two days are when you should log all your content—giving the impression you've spent your entire vacation at said resort, when in fact you've only been there a night. This is a real money saver.)

What I also remember about that night at the Four Seasons in Hawaii all those years ago is that I realized I did not want to be with the person I was with anymore. (This person that I said I was not going to mention again in this essay. That I have twice since.) I realized that I was unhappy, and no amount of vacation could fix that. No beautiful resort or ocean view or free breakfast could change anything.

I never planned to write about this when I started this essay. I never planned to write about this relationship at all. It is not fun or festive or very vacation-y: a breakup in Hawaii. But it's what happened. It's almost worse to be lonely with another person someplace so beautiful than it is to be lonely with another person at home. At least that's what I discovered on that trip to Hawaii. Everything is magnified when you're away from home. No job or errands or friends to hide behind. To make you think what's happening isn't really happening. You are left with only the other person.

Leaving the bed-and-breakfast for our night at the Four Seasons, I felt excited, as if the hotel would somehow make things better. As if I would be happy there. And of course, as often happens in these situations, it had the opposite effect. It was too beautiful a place to be unhappy in. Too beautiful to be sharing with someone I did not want to share it with, did not want to be with.

We Are Experiencing a Slight Delay

The funny thing is, on the first date I had with this person I was on the Hawaii trip with, I thought, *No, not for me.* But then he did something kind, and I thought, *I can't believe I was so quick to write this person off. To not give this person a chance.* It took me four years to realize that I was correct on that very first date. No, not for me. And I had to go five thousand miles to the Four Seasons on the Big Island of Hawaii to realize I was sitting at dinner on the beach with the wrong person. While stretching one day into two. When all I really wanted was to go home.

Never take a trip with someone you don't want to be with. I guess that's two tips.

I've never felt like I needed to be with another person. I didn't think I'd ever meet a partner that I would share so much of my life with, like I eventually did.

Years later, I go back to that same resort with Brad. We have a wonderful time. When possible, always change bad memories to good ones. Now that's *three* tips.

chapter fifteen

Australia

Day
1

I'm in Australia. I just arrived in Melbourne today at 6:00 a.m. It is now 7:00 p.m., and I'm sitting in my hotel room, waiting to go to dinner. This has possibly been the longest day of my life. Landing in a country at 6:00 a.m. after flying fifteen hours is ungodly. What are we supposed to do with that? Also, it's a day later. And it's spring here, even though it's fall everywhere else (okay, MOST everywhere). At this point they could tell me tomorrow was Christmas, and I'd be like, "Sure, whatever."

I'm here alone because I'm doing shows in Melbourne and

We Are Experiencing a Slight Delay

Sydney. Actually, "show" feels like too strong a word. Like it may be promising far more than I deliver. Like *Hamilton* is a show. So I try to lower expectations as much as possible by, first of all, NOT calling it a show. I can't say "experience," because that's even worse. I don't call it a reading because that sounds kind of dull. Hence an "evening-ish," which sounds about right. I'm not taking up a whole evening. Just a smidge. And I am mostly reading from my two books, but also there's other stuff. Anyway, that's why I'm here. Brad had to stay home and work, so it's just me.

What seemed like a good idea six months ago now has me a bit nervous. Six months ago, I would have said yes to hang gliding off the Empire State Building. Six months ago, I would have said yes to anything, because six months in the future is forever away. But of course it's not. It's actually almost today. I have no idea how this is going to go. Saturday in Melbourne, I have two "shows": one at night, and then an added matinee because the evening show sold out. The matinee, though, has not. And unlike Patti LuPone when she was performing in *Evita*, I do not have an understudy to cover matinees. I just hope it goes well. "Goes down a treat," as the Brits say (do Aussies say this, too?).

Brad and I have been to Australia before. I love it here. I've been dying to come back, and this seemed like a great way to do it. The thing I like about Australia is how far removed it is from everything. It's really out on its own. I kind of feel like that as a person sometimes. Like I'm the human embodiment of Australia. Off on my own, and fine with it. So I'm excited to be here, but honestly also nervous. The only way I can write about this is knowing that by the time you read this, it will be over.

Today, on what has thus far been the longest day of my life (and I still have dinner to go to!), I took a bike from my hotel and rode through the Botanic Gardens (which you're not supposed to do on a bike) and I stopped and took an Instagram story of some birds I came upon.

I was then sent hundreds of DMs saying that these birds were vicious magpies, and that it being spring and all, it was swooping season, and they were going to try to kill me. I thought maybe this was a prank, but on reviewing the accompanying videos sent to me of people being terrorized by these birds (the ones of children being attacked by far the funniest), I realized it was true. Apparently, the mother birds are protecting their nests, and I guess every so often they poke out someone's eye as they ride by on their bike. Anyplace else this would be horrible, but it feels right for Australia.

Also, I just love Australians. It's impossible for me not to smile while talking to one of them. Every word is abbreviated, from "brekkie" to "avro" (for afternoon, I don't get that one), except short words, which are all the length of a motion picture. "Yeaaaaaaaaaaaaaaaaaaaaaaah." "Noooooooooooooor."

We Are Experiencing a Slight Delay

Tonight I'm going to dinner alone at a new buzzy spot called Reine & La Rue. The exact type of restaurant you would NOT want to go to alone. But since I'm roughly in the ninety-seventh hour of this day, I feel like, why not? I will not be dining alone at a table for two, as I wrote about in a previous essay. I will be sitting at the counter. And I'm bringing a book along with my phone. I need a few crutches tonight, to ease myself into the trip.

Oh, and twice today I went into the drugstore on the corner where my hotel is. (They say "chemist." Cute.) I'm always in drugstores when I travel, for some reason. I've forgotten at least ten things that I slowly accumulate as I remember each one. And the woman working there, Sue, was so kind, and we chatted for a while. I'm always very chatty when I'm newly arrived. I want to go into the drugstore now every day, just to say hi to Sue. I'm sure I forgot more stuff anyway. Today it was shaving cream and a US adapter for my electric beard trimmer. (No chance I was ever going to remember that one.)

It was chilly today, but I didn't mind. I'm also very aware of my American accent, since so far I've only heard Australian ones.

I might write a little each day. Or I might not. Let's just see how this goes. I'm stressed out enough about the two shows on Saturday, without any additional pressure.

One more thing: I just looked at the menu at Reine & La Rue. I'm worried.

Day
2

Okay, dinner last night was fun. The restaurant beautiful (an old bank, maybe?). I went alone, but two women who had DMed me on Instagram (and also helped me with restaurant reservations in Australia) came by and had a drink with me. Actually, they had a drink, and I had my dinner.

This is normally something I would hate, but I didn't—it was lovely. I didn't tell them this, but I will tell you. I was a bit lonely last night. Sometimes, when I least expect it, old feelings come up. Being thirteen again. Eating alone in the library again. That sort of thing. Normally, I like eating alone—being alone. I have no problem with it. But last night, well . . . it was nice that something unexpected happened. I went from looking at my phone at the counter to sitting at a table with Megan and Jo who I had previously only known through my phone. A moment of connection. And the food was delicious. I had the fish.

This morning I did a radio show, where a lovely woman, Chrissie Swan, kindly made me blueberry muffins that I dissected live on her show. I'm not going to lie, sometimes I feel insane. Why am I in Australia, cutting open muffins on the radio (where you can't even see the results)? If you are reading this and not aware that I cut open blueberry muffins on my Instagram, well, then it's kind of hard to explain. But the upshot is, it leaves me at times feeling a bit mad. Sometimes we can't explain the things we do and why they have the results they do. But it was another moment of connection.

Later, my friend Gus from Sydney came, and we walked together all afternoon. He's here to support me and see my shows tomorrow. I told him I was anxious about it, and now I'm thinking maybe I shouldn't have said anything. Like, he flew here to see me; did I need to tell him I was anxious? Sometimes pretending everything is okay is easier. Now I'm maybe making myself *more* anxious by talking about how anxious I am, so I'm going to stop that.

But I am super anxious. I'm in my hotel room, listening to the birds outside, as I write this. It's Friday afternoon, and the street I'm on is lined with cafés and restaurants. Everyone is outside drinking and talking. Normally, this is a sound that I like. The sound of a sunny Friday afternoon sidewalk café conversation, from a terrace several stories above. But now I'm too nervous to enjoy it.

I am supposed to leave shortly to be a guest on a TV show here called *The Project*. I have no idea what it is, or what I'm supposed to be doing on it. If I were at home and about to go on, say, *Live with Kelly and Mark*, I would be more nervous because, well, I know what that is. It's like a real thing. But something you don't know, have never heard of, will never see, is a lot easier somehow. It kind of points out how ridiculous everything is. How we are all playing these parts, but it's all kind of nonsense. A bit of pretend. So at least I'm not quite as nervous about this show that I've never heard of, starring people that I don't know, that I will never watch. Nor will anyone else I know.

After I film this show, I'm meeting Gus for dinner. We're going to a restaurant I booked five months ago, because apparently that's how popular it is. I mean, how good can any restaurant be anyway? I just want a well-done burger.

I'm kind of nervous to go to bed tonight, knowing I have to wake up tomorrow and do two shows. My stomach is flipping as I type this. The thing that makes me feel a bit better is that at least I flew to Australia to see the audience, and they didn't fly to LA to see me. Everyone I've met so far has been so warm and kind and funny and lovely. There it is again—tiny moments of connection. Blink and you might miss them.

I almost forgot, I went to the drugstore to get electric clippers because mine shorted today while trimming my beard, and Sue wasn't there. Apparently, the US-to-Australia adapter thing caused some kind of tiny explosion in my electric beard clipper. They didn't have one, though. So I have to go to another drugstore tomorrow. The woman that was there today told me I should take the tram to a larger drugstore in another part of town. As I was nodding, I already knew I wasn't going to do it. I wonder what Sue would have told me.

Okay, I have to go get dressed for this stupid talk show. Wish me luck tomorrow.

Day
4

I'm in Sydney now. There is a big rivalry between Melbourne and Sydney. I'm going to do my best to remain neutral, but I already feel like the Melburnians are going to be mad at me, because I think Sydney is really gorgeous. I'm going to have to be muted in the way I talk about Sydney in order not to offend Melbourne, my newly adopted city.

Right now, I'm sitting in my hotel room writing this and looking out over the Sydney Harbour and directly at the opera house. It's truly stunning. One of the most beautiful views in the—I mean, it's fine. You've seen one view, you've seen them all.

A really great thing happened yesterday. I woke up, and I wasn't anxious. It was gone. I had two shows, and people came from different parts of Australia, and I read from my books and I answered questions. I met hundreds of people, and it was wonderful. As anxious as I was the day before the shows, that's how *not* anxious I was yesterday. You know how when you hear it said that you need to "find your people"? Well, I found them, and they're all in Australia.

If you've never been here, I can't recommend it enough. The first thing I will tell you, though, is don't go to Starbucks while in Melbourne. Don't even mention it, just to be safe. My entire time there I had it only once and I'm still doing damage control. If you haven't heard that Melbourne has the best coffee in the world (and they do), don't worry, they'll tell you. Repeatedly.

I guess I wasn't aware how seriously they took their coffee. I think if had drowned a kitten on my Instagram story, I would've gotten less outrage than I did from walking into a Starbucks in Melbourne. But I now realize my mistake, and will not make it again. I tell you this as a warning, reader. In every other way, the Melburnians are the most warm, friendly, fabulous people you will ever meet. But do not fuck with their coffee, or they will drag you. (I mean, it's not like I put the Starbucks there, but whatever.)

I invited the front desk staff of the hotel I was staying in, United Places, to my show. I feel weird asking if people want to come, because then I feel like they'll feel obligated. I know what a nightmare that would be for me, so I don't want to do it to anybody else. But I invited them anyway, and Cara and Tamara from the front desk came last night. I was so happy to see them after the show. It's weird that something so little can mean so much. "You came!" I said when I saw them backstage afterward. I had known them for three days, but when I saw them, it was like I had friends at the show.

A connection, a friendship, a relationship, does not have to last forever. We don't have to follow each other on social media for years, or DM, or text or see each other ever again. It can be for just three days. It can exist within that time span only. No use trying to extend it or repeat it or belabor it. But for three days, we are in each other's lives. And they came! It made me happy.

My friend Gus was there, too, and he brought a friend, and some Australian boys Brad and I met this summer in Mykonos came. We went to dinner after, to what is now one of my favorite restaurants, France-Soir. And I ate for the first time that day. The best omelet I can remember ever having eaten. And in that moment, everything was perfect.

My show in Sydney is on Wednesday, but I'm not anxious anymore. I hope it doesn't come back. You can never be sure, though. I'm looking at the light from the sunset hitting the opera house now, and it is the most—basic thing I've ever seen. Nothing like the Melbourne (pronounced Melbn) Botanic (called the Tan) Garden. Now, *that's* a view.

I'm going to stay in tonight and watch TV and order room service. I can't hear the sound of my own voice anymore. A little of me goes a long way, I find.

Oh, and I still didn't get any clippers to trim my beard. And I went back to that drugstore in Melbourne once more, but never saw Sue again.

Day
6

I ended up watching *The Exorcist* and then *Billy Elliot* the other night. It made for the most fucked-up double feature I'd ever seen. Whenever Billy was dancing, I kept thinking he was possessed by the devil. Then I was like, *Oh, wait, that's not him—that's the other kid.* I was so freaked out from *The Exorcist* (why is that still so terrifying?) that I couldn't fall asleep until I saw Billy get into ballet school. It still didn't erase the image of Linda Blair speaking in tongues and shoving her mother's face into her privates, though; it just ruined *Billy Elliot*. One of my favorite feel-good movies is now forever conflated with satanic possession in my mind. Great.

Yesterday, I planned to sleep in, but I didn't because see above. The weather was gorgeous (don't read the rest of this, Melbourne), and I took the ferry to the Taronga Zoo. The Sydney Harbour is really one of the most beautiful harbors in the world. And there are ferries that take you everywhere.

They depart like buses from the ferry terminal. For around a dollar, you can basically go on a cruise. (Not unlike Carnival Cruise Line.)

I've been wanting to see koalas since I got here. I went to the Taronga Zoo with Brad the first time we came to Australia, seventeen years ago. (This is actually my third time here. People keep acting as if I've never been to Australia before, and I'm like, "Yeah, I've been to Bondi Beach, I've done that walk, what else ya got?") But I hadn't been back to the zoo since that first trip, and I really wanted to see the koalas again.

The zoo is directly across the harbor, so you can look at giraffes while seeing the water and the skyline just beyond. It's really one of the most spectacular city views you'll ever see. (I told you not to read this part, Melbourne!) While I was walking around, one of the zookeepers (do they still call them zookeepers?), Mel, recognized me from Instagram. (She technically recognized me from Brad's Instagram, not mine, but still.)

Mel then took me around on a little private tour, and we got to go backstage to see the animals. Then she took me right into the area where the koalas are, and I had a private audience with them. She explained tons of stuff about koalas to me, most of which I've already forgotten, except the fact that after they eat, it takes them an entire week to shit it out. That I'll never forget. It's one of the best facts

I've ever learned about a marsupial. (Also, they're not ko-ala bears, they're just koalas. Don't make my mistake.) It was the best hour I've had since I can remember. I know I thanked you in person, Mel, but now I'm thanking you in a book. That's got to count for something. Also, Mel is coming to my show tomorrow night, so really I've more than repaid the favor, Mel.

Still haven't been anxious again, so I'm really happy about that. Today I went on two morning shows. I think they have like ten morning shows here. I was also invited to be on a popular quiz show, but then uninvited, so I'm kind of wondering what I did to cause them to revoke the invitation (probably say "koala bear"), but also kind of glad. I'm sure I wouldn't have known anything they asked me, unless it was "How long after eating does it take for a koala to shit out its food?"

I'm nervous about my show tomorrow night, but not to a crippling extent. I don't even think *I'd* go to see me, so I'm always very flattered when people show up. Maybe I should ask Cara and Tamara from the United Places Hotel in Melbourne to fly up, so I have some more friends in the audience.

Having dinner with Gus tonight. He is my guide to all things Australian. Particularly drinking. Which they like very much. He wants me to go on the Harbour Bridge climb with him, but I am terrified of heights. Apparently, you climb along the very top of the bridge, which just seems stupid. He penciled it in for Friday. I said, "Light pencil, please." Everyone keeps telling me how easy it is, that senior citizens and children do it, but somehow that doesn't make me feel any better. I'll keep you posted. I can only get through one terrifying thing at a time.

Finally, found clippers to trim my beard at a nearby drugstore. Nobody chatted me up like in Melbourne. It was simply a business transaction. I also passed a wash-and-fold laundry, so I know where to bring my clothes tomorrow. I think walking with my dirty laundry to the local wash-and-fold will really settle my nerves before the show. Common everyday chores have always had a way of calming me. If I could empty a dishwasher, I'd really be set. Maybe I'll just ask the hotel to let me change the sheets on the bed.

I got Starbucks today. Sydney doesn't give a shit.

Day
8

Yesterday I started my day by walking with my laundry to the local wash-and-fold, and it really centered me for my show. I also went to the Art Gallery of NSW. It was fabulous. I must have spent at least an hour there. I like a museum that's not filled with tourists, and this was one of them. I always head straight to the cafeteria first. I like to think of museums as coffee shops with really expensive art. "Wow, this café has a room of Rembrandts in it!" It makes the museum seem less overwhelming and the coffee shop more impressive.

After an hour looking at art, I headed back to the hotel to get ready for the show. The weather was perfect, which was good for me since my mood is directly affected by sunlight. An overcast day would've sent me into a downward spiral I might not have come out of.

The audience in Sydney was incredible last night, and they brought me tons of muffins to try (unlike you, Melbourne), but the muffins did not go down a treat. There is something about a blueberry muffin that gets lost in translation here. It's like the Stepford Wives: they might look like the real thing, but something's definitely off. During the Q and A part of the show, someone asked me, "What's your favorite animal?" and someone else when called upon just randomly did a birdcall until I had to stop them, so in this particular arena, Melbourne really outshone its rival. I met several mother-daughter teams, which are always my favorite. And Mel from the zoo came! I was so happy to see her; she was my Cara and Tamara in Sydney. If I lived in Sydney, I would definitely be friends with Mel.

We Are Experiencing a Slight Delay

I asked everyone I met who was coming to the show to stop backstage for a drink after. Gus brought his sister Amelia, who I instantly liked. It's always nice when you meet a friend's sibling for the first time. Another piece of the puzzle. But I left early and came back to the hotel, and had a club sandwich from room service and watched *House Hunters*. It was the British version, and the woman didn't pick a house at the end. She's "going to keep thinking," she tells the real estate agent. What the fuck?

I went to bed, wondering why I bothered watching this woman look at three houses in Gloucestershire if she wasn't going to buy one. This would never fly in America.

Today I went to Bondi Beach with Gus and we went swimming. I did not get eaten by a shark, but was mentally prepared for the possibility. He said people don't get eaten at that beach, but I didn't believe him. I think he just wanted me to go in the water and take my chances like the rest of them. Then we went on this really incredible walk that everyone will tell you to take if you ever go to Sydney (see day six), and didn't finish it. It was nice to not have to be nervous any longer, so I finally had the bandwidth to ask Gus a question. He was in *The Great Gatsby*, directed by Baz Luhrmann. He told me what that was like. His character is named Teddy Barton. I'm going to watch it again to see him. You would like Gus, I think. He is what we call a good egg. I know several good eggs, Brad being the goodest.

Tomorrow I have promised Gus I will do the Harbour Bridge climb, even though I'm terrified. He keeps insisting that children as young as four have done it, but Australians are not like regular people. There's nothing in this country that won't try to kill you, so a toddler scaling the outer structure of a bridge is not a big deal. It's probably got a better chance of surviving that than brushing its teeth. I'm sure they have some kind of microscopic water spider that comes out of the tap and shoots poison into your gums. I'm afraid I'm going to chicken out at the last minute, though. I can't even look up at the top of the Harbour Bridge from my hotel without holding on to something. Also, you have to leave your phone with them at the bottom of the bridge, and can't film it, so why bother? I guess I'll sleep on it.

Oh, they just lit the Sydney Opera House! I wish you could see it!

Day
9

I'm waiting for Gus to pick me up for the bridge climb. I'm nervous, but planning to do it. It's another beautiful day, so that's a big motivator. I watched another British *House*

Hunters before going to bed last night, and the couple ac-tually bought the house, so I considered that a good omen.

Tonight we are going to see the final performance of *Miss Saigon* at the opera house, so at least I have something to live for.

I think I have enough time to run to Starbucks before Gus gets here. (Don't tell Melbourne.) I know I'm going to have to pee now once I get to the top.

Day
10

I did it. I won't lie, it was a bit terrifying. But sometimes it's more exhausting expending the energy on *not* doing something than just getting it over with. (Like writing this book.) This was one of those instances.

Our guide, Tanner, was great. He was telling us about kids doing the climb who pooped themselves out of fear, and that really set the right tone. It's hard to be afraid when you're laughing. Also, by doing the bridge climb, I could finally shut Gus up.

While at the top, they shot a video for us, so it was nice to be able to log a little content from up there. I didn't conquer my fear of heights, though. I don't think it works like that.

You just have to push through the fear. Not unlike most things, except this one also has the potential of hitting the ground and exploding like a watermelon.

Miss Saigon was terrific (even though we got a Kim understudy. Thankfully, I didn't find out till intermission, and I was already on board with her journey at that point). Also, it was really time in this trip for a musical. (The thing about traveling is to always know when to slot things in.)

Afterward, Gus took me out dancing in the gay part of Darlinghurst. If the gay neighborhood *wasn't* in the place named Darlinghurst, the Sydney gays would have made a terrible mistake. But they got it right. I have maybe one night out in me per ten-day trip, and the perfect night for that is always the second-to-last day of the trip. The day when you're up for anything, and in the full bloom of your trip potential. The last day of the trip is for mentally extracting yourself from your fake life and reinserting yourself into your real one. But the day before that is basically fucking Mardi Gras.

We went to two clubs, breaking my rule of "never let them take you to a second location," but what can I say? Gus is a persuasive ambassador for his city. The first club was called Universal, and was on two floors. I spent most of my time there trying to locate persons who were older than myself. Thankfully, there were a few. At forty-two, Gus is a good bridge between the twenty-something twinks there and me. That's why I always like to go out with someone in their forties. (Brad fits this bill nicely, and Gus did excellent understudy work. Not unlike our Kim this evening.) The eye needs to settle on something between twenty-five and fifty-five, otherwise it's just too startling. I am wise enough to recognize this.

I was at the upstairs part of the club while Gus was downstairs getting drinks. When he finds me again, he tells me that I just missed Kylie Minogue's "Padam Padam." I am devastated, since Kylie is the only singer I want to hear while in Australia. (And really one of the incentives to going out was being able to dance to Kylie in her motherland with her Aussie gays. Missing this song will be one of my great life regrets.) At about 1:00 a.m., I'm pretty much ready to go, and Gus asks if we can make one more stop. (This is when I break my rule of "never let them take you to a second location.") I demur, but again, I can't emphasize enough how persuasive Gus can be, and how infectious his energy is, so I say sure. Also, he's tall, and tall people can get you to do stuff more easily than regular-size people, I've found. (Remember, this is the second-to-last night of the trip, and I'm basically an Australian citizen at this point. Game for all of it. Fully in. Today, writing this on my final day here, all I can think of are my dogs and my bed, but last night was a completely different story.)

We walk a few blocks along Oxford Street, which looks

remarkably similar to Santa Monica Boulevard, to a small bar called Palms.

We go downstairs into the cramped, bare-bones, sticky-carpeted room. And the tiny space is filled with a cross section of the entire gay community. Everyone is represented, and they are friendly and smiling and drinking beer, and dancing to Whitney Houston and Madonna and Dolly Parton (sadly, no Kylie). Gus and I weave our way into the middle of the floor and join the crowd, now a part of it, absorbed by it. Both smiling, happy. Not having to say a word because we each know what the other is thinking. Sometimes you just know you're exactly where you should be. In a basement in Sydney on a Friday night dancing with Gus.

He is picking me up at my hotel in a few minutes. We are going to a gallery, and then a boat ride and a final dinner. I won't tell him I'm thinking of Brad and my dogs and my bed. That I already have mentally left Australia, am already home. But he will know.

chapter sixteen

The Orient Express

Brad and I have just returned from a trip on the Orient Express.

This is one of those trips that you think is going to be one thing, but ends up being another. Like what could be more glamorous than the Orient Express? Turns out, a lot of stuff. First off, the train is stunning. An exact replica of the 1920s *Venice Simplon-Orient-Express*. The one that rose to fame from the Agatha Christie novel *Murder on the Orient Express*, which, as far as titles go, is right up there with *To Kill a Mockingbird* and the Bible.

We were invited to host a charity event on board, and

We Are Experiencing a Slight Delay

I couldn't be more excited. The train instantly conjures images of glamour and intrigue not seen since, well, the 1920s—which, so far, seem a hell of a lot more fun than the 2020s have been. I imagine train cars snaking through snow-covered mountain passes, scenery that makes you gasp and reach for your camera, or stare out at it thoughtfully as a single tear rolls down your cheek, so moved are you by its sheer beauty. Gaping out the window for hours as if watching your own private National Geographic special. Making your way to the dining car in your tux, a blur of postcard-worthy landscapes whizzing by, as you slosh the champagne in your glass and steady yourself on a mahogany handrail. Yeah, well, this wasn't that.

Let's see, how to explain . . . Have you ever taken the Metro-North? Or the LIRR? Or any commuter rail service, where you stop every few miles at local nondescript train stations? Well, imagine doing that for twenty-four hours in formal wear. If there was a station between Paris and Venice we didn't pull up to, I would be surprised. It's hard to be transported back in time when every thirty minutes you're watching people with briefcases and backpacks stare into the window at the idiots sipping martinis, dressed like extras in a James Bond casino scene. It's not dissimilar, I imagine, to lining up in a convention center, dressed as Mr. Spock or Chewbacca.

The Orient Express

What was going to be a Met Gala on wheels feels like cheap cosplay when seen through the eyes of those dressed appropriately for the garishly lit suburban train station at 5:00 p.m. It's asking a lot of people to suspend their disbelief while eating in tuxedos and evening gowns, parked directly across from a train station McDonald's for an hour. If you can see someone in sweats biting into a Big Mac on the other side of the glass, it makes it a bit difficult to lose yourself in the romance of a bygone era.

"I feel like a fucking idiot," I say to Brad while sipping from a crystal water glass in clothes more appropriate for the Oscars.

"We look ridiculous," Brad agrees, waving back at someone on the platform holding a grocery bag while gawking at us like penguins in the zoo.

I guess we had to be rerouted due to work on the tracks or weather, or something like that. Who knew there were so many shitty train stations between Paris and Venice? I've been on subway rides that stopped less frequently. During the late evening, we're actually stuck at one for at least four hours.

At dinner, we sit with an attractive young couple we've just met. The first thing I ask is, "Did you think the train would be stopping this much?" They respond, "No!"

Two gentlemen at the next table overhear us (I mean,

it's a train; how far apart are the tables going to be? They might as well be sitting on my lap). They say, "We had no idea, either!"

These people weren't going to mention anything about it, but once I get the ball rolling, the whole dining car is eager to join in.

"Where are the mountains?"

"I know!! Or anything!!"

A release of tension occurs, now that we can discuss the elephant in the train. Nothing bonds people more quickly than disappointment. In no time at all, everyone is complaining like old friends. I have to admit, it's nice. Dissatisfaction ends up being the perfect icebreaker. Stripping away our pretenses and polite veneers allows us to actually have normal conversations. Joking, laughing, bitching. Short of somebody getting murdered, this ends up being the most happy outcome for the evening.

Back in our cabin later that night, Brad and I change into our natty pajamas while gazing out over the fluorescent lights of a KFC.

"I do feel like I'm being transported back in time," I say. "Back to the time when I could only afford fast food."

The next morning, our incredible steward, Noé, brings us our breakfast as we watch the Brutalist apartment complexes and parking lots go by. If we passed a patch of green, I must have been in the bathroom for it. Having introduced myself to everybody on the train the day before, I now have to avoid everyone this morning. It's like bumping into someone at the valet after you've already said good night at the party. But on a train.

At a certain point, I just want to hide in our cabin until we arrive in Venice. If you've had one nice moment with a stranger, best to leave it at that, I say. All the charm I've had in me has already been leached out at this point. What you are going to get now is the personality equivalent of coffee grinds at the bottom of a mug. All the good stuff is gone.

(I wonder how many of them I followed last night on Instagram in a moment of weakness. I've already followed far too many people over the years, and now I have no idea who the fuck they are. One impetuous tap of the phone, and I'm following at least a hundred people's lives who I maybe have ever known for thirty minutes over several glasses of wine. Now I can't bring myself to unfollow them. Even after many years. I'm stuck watching some random kid go from high school to college, just because I may have exchanged a pleasantry with their mom in 2017.)

But I rally and leave the cabin (compartment?) and make my rounds, my good mornings, my good afternoons, my how was your nights, my how is your days. A lunch in the dining car. Smiles, glasses clinking; a bit more subdued today, everyone slowly retreating, wrapping things up. Once again, Brad and I are back in our room. Folding suits and jackets and sweaters.

Our steward Noé (who is so wonderful, and leaves us the most lovely note before we depart) stops by and asks for our key. Our suite is named "Paris," and the key has a tiny Eiffel Tower on its chain. Strangely, we cannot find it. We scour every inch of the small space, but nothing. Which is odd, because I never lose keys. I always put them in the exact same place, so as not to forget their location. (Brad, on the other hand, is the opposite. "Have you seen my keys?" is a frequent refrain. He will disagree with me, but I am right. If he'd like to rebut this, he can write his own goddamn book.) I feel bad that we have lost it. That Noé might think we have taken it on purpose as a souvenir. That we are lying. Either way, it is gone.

The final bit of the trip, Brad and I spend alone in our compartment. Noé has already taken our bags (there is no one with less luggage on this train than us), and we sit in the perfect little suite, at the perfect little table. So much of our lives we have spent together now. So many trains and planes and boats and cars. Comings and goings, hellos and goodbyes, to so many people in so many places over so many years. And the one constant is Brad. Who I met on a trip, not unlike this one, so long ago. Who walked by me in a restaurant. Who I said hello to. Who came back to my room. Then back to my home. Who has been with me through everything since that night in that taverna when I said, "I'm Gary. What's your name?"

Suddenly, the train turns a bend, and in the last minutes, all of Venice is laid out before us. The sun is low in the sky, reflecting on the water. It's so beautiful, and it goes by so quickly.

In our hotel, late that night, I open my toiletries case and there, underneath the toothpaste and the shaving cream, is a key chain with a tiny Eiffel tower. It must have found its way in somehow. In that moment, I decide I will keep it in this case forever.

"Look what I found," I say, holding it up to Brad.

chapter seventeen

Favorites

(Because people ask me. There are tons of other fabulous options, I know. These are just a few.)

New York

THE MERCER HOTEL. Been staying here for twenty years. Never goes out of fashion. If you want to feel like you have an apartment in the city, this is the place. Lovely staff. Home.

BACCARAT HOTEL. A new favorite. Fabulous. Get a room facing Fifty-third Street. Go to afternoon tea.

BALTHAZAR. Everyone goes to Balthazar, and it's always good. Shrimp cocktail and burger. My first night in New York is always Balthazar.

POLO BAR. I know it's hard to get into, but go when you can get a reservation. After theater is great. It also has Nelly, the best, most fabulous, head maître d' in all of New York. I get the burger here, too. And the coconut cake for dessert.

JOE ALLEN. Best restaurant for before or after the theater, hands-down. Burger again.

RAOUL'S. SoHo bistro that will instantly make you feel like a New Yorker. You can only get the burger at the bar, and they only make twelve per night. Which makes you want it that much more (obviously). I do chicken and fries here.

I SODI. My favorite Italian. Get the lasagna.

DON ANGIE. My other favorite Italian

London

THE CHILTERN FIREHOUSE. Perhaps my favourite hotel. (British spelling for all my London favourites.) The staff, led by Hamish and David, is the best I've ever encountered. Sometimes I spend an evening hanging out at the front desk with a glass of wine, and then just rambling around the hotel, chatting to various people. Those are the best nights. Get a room facing Chiltern Street. The smallest ones that have a fireplace are fabulous.

J. SHEEKEY. My London Balthazar. I can't leave the city until I've been once. Always after theatre. And always fish and chips and mushy peas.

BOUCHON RACINE. A new favourite. The best roast chicken. It's like you've stepped into Paris. The most charming, simple room. What all restaurants should feel like.

BARRAFINA. The original is in Soho. Only counter seating. Always busy. Super casual and delicious. I came here alone at least once a week while I was living in London, working on *Vicious*. Have a glass of Rioja and *pan con tomate* while you wait. That's what I do, anyway. It really makes the time fly.

TRISHNA. My favourite Indian restaurant.

THE DELAUNAY. Go for lunch. Gorgeous room.

CLARIDGE'S. No better afternoon tea in the city. Make sure you're in the main room. If they try to put you in the side room, say, "Gary says I'm supposed to sit in the main room, not this one."

THE MONOCLE CAFÉ. This is where I get my coffee every day on Chiltern Street. My favourite street in London. Don't tell everyone, though. It's just for you guys reading my book.

MONMOUTH COFFEE. Go to the one on Monmouth Street. My second-favourite coffee and second-favourite street. (Where the Covent Garden Hotel is, too. I still haven't been back inside, BTW.)

THE GRAPES. Ian McKellen's pub in Limehouse. It's one of the oldest, most homely (that means "homey" to them. I know, weird) pubs in London, and has the best pub quiz every Monday. On a summer night, you can have your pint on the tiny back terrace directly on the Thames. Heaven.

See what's on at the NATIONAL THEATRE and pick something. Walk there. I bet you can from wherever you're staying. It's the most wonderful spot.

Paris

Stay anywhere. It's Paris. But I love LE BRISTOL.

CHEZ ANDRÉ. Paris Balthazar. Get the lentils. Then the roast chicken and frites (they don't call them *pommes frites*, just *frites*, FYI) and profiteroles. And they have the cutest half bottles of Sancerre. It's the perfect meal. Totally casual, not pricey. And you, like, *know* you're in Paris. Which is what you want when you're in Paris. I don't want sushi in Paris; I can get that in LA. (And I don't want to stay in a Bali-inspired hotel. I want my hotel room to look Balinese when I'm in Bali. Not Paris. My biggest pet peeve is when you're staying at a hotel in another country that looks like a different country from the one you're visiting. I want where I'm staying to look like where I'm staying. France should look French, Italy should look Italian, etc. If I wanted a Japanese-inspired hotel I would go to Japan, not Venice.)

LE PETIT LUTETIA. If you like rice pudding (I love it), this is your spot. Everything else is also delicious.

LE VOLTAIRE. I like this place, too.

LA FONTAINE DE MARS. And this one. Love the outdoor courtyard.

I also like Starbucks in Paris. They have some good ones.

(Whatever you do, don't tell Melbourne I said that.)

Also, go to the movies in Paris. Nobody makes a peep. It will be the quietest cinema you've ever been in.

Go to the sculpture garden at the MUSÉE RODIN. It's gorgeous, outside, and you're in and out in under an hour.

Rome

HOTEL DE RUSSIE. My favorite. It has an outdoor courtyard and beautiful gardens. Most gorgeous setting for breakfast. I love a good hotel breakfast. This one is right up there.

DAL BOLOGNESE. Just outside the hotel on the Piazza del Popolo. You definitely want to eat outside facing the piazza, one of Rome's most beautiful. If they try to put you inside, complain bitterly like I did.

Go to Trastevere. We liked the pasta at ZI UMBERTO. Super charming. (You're definitely in Italy here. Which we love. See Chez André above.)

Loved the pizza at BONCI PIZZARIUM. Get a ticket and wait on line. Then you sit on the curb and eat it. Can't recommend it enough. (It's near the Vatican, so knock that off your list, too.)

My coffee place is SANT'EUSTACHIO. Get the granita con panna. Fabio should be working. Say hi.

Venice

GRITTI PALACE. One of the most beautiful hotels I've ever stayed at. It's expensive, so this is a splurge. (This is a good hotel in which to use the one-night travel tip, BTW.) Get a room facing the Grand Canal. The hotel has the most amazing deck on the canal, where you have breakfast and can get aperitivos in the evening. All of Venice will pass you by here. You literally don't have to leave the hotel. (Which are always my favorite kind of hotels.)

DA IVO. Delicious. And George Clooney had his bachelor party here. If it's good enough for George Clooney . . .

Go to the PEGGY GUGGENHEIM COLLECTION museum. Again, all you need is an hour. Not even. And it's fabulous.

Take a vaporetto everywhere. It's like their subway, but on the water and way better.

Venice should be on the top of everyone's travel list. It will never disappoint. (Go off season if it's your first time.)

Rio

Rio is one of my favorite cities in the world. I was actually there just before I started writing this book. Brad and I were filming a travel show there, and then . . . you know, that thing happened where everything shut down. The most wonderful beaches, architecture, food, people. Go!

HOTEL FASANO. Another expensive one that's worth the splurge. Right on Ipanema Beach. Best rooftop pool I've ever been to. All of Rio is laid out in front of you. I love the rooms, the staff. If you're not staying here, come for a drink on the roof at sunset. (In an episode of *Family Guy* that I wrote, Stewie goes on about this hotel in a monologue in the episode "Send in Stewie, Please." Even *he* knows this is the place to stay in Rio.)

APRAZIVEL. In Santa Teresa. You eat in tree houses with a view of the city. It's pretty fucking great.

LASAI. Brad and I loved this restaurant. We filmed here for the travel show you will never see, and had our favorite meal of the trip at this restaurant. The food is local and from their gardens. Best tasting menu ever. Also, they're all lovely.

POLIS SUCOS. It's a juice bar just off the beach in Ipanema. You order at a counter. Best açai juice and grilled cheese sandwiches. Everyone goes after the beach. Just stand and eat. Don't miss it.

COPACABANA PALACE. Go on Saturday for the *feijoada*. It's basically like their version of brunch or Sunday roast, but a million times better.

CORCOVADO. Take the little train up. Iconic.

Melbourne

UNITED PLACES HOTEL. One of my favorite small hotels. Right across the street from the Botanic Gardens in the most charming neighborhood. Rooms are like little apartments, and everyone who works there is lovely. (Hi, Cara, Tamara, and Nate!) I wouldn't stay anywhere else in Melbourne. And they have bikes!

GILSON. A few doors down from the hotel. This basically served as my hotel lobby and restaurant while I was in Melbourne. When I wasn't in my room, I was in Gilson. Fantastic coffee. Great staff. Breakfast till late. I wish I had a Gilson here.

ST. ALI. Also, great coffee and great food. I loved St. Ali. I also wish I had one in LA. (Did I mention that Melbourne is known for its coffee?)

FRANCE-SOIR. My favorite restaurant in Melbourne. It's like you've stepped into Paris. (Which goes against everything I've said above. "You want to feel like you've stepped into Paris when you're in Paris, blah blah"—but this is the exception that proves the rule.) Beautiful bistro. You can tell it's a part of the city; that it's an institution. The food was also delicious. And I won't lie: there's something neat about being in Australia and feeling like you're in Paris. If I lived in Melbourne, I would be here once a week.

Sydney

PARK HYATT. Another splurge, but there is no other hotel I would stay in. I mean, you're all the way in fucking Australia! You want to look out on the harbor and the opera house. And every room has a terrace! And there's a pool on the roof! And breakfast is included! And you can take a water taxi right from the hotel! I could go on.

10 WILLIAM STREET. Great Italian restaurant and wine bar. Total neighborhood place. Near Gus's house. Get the pretzel! After drinks and snacks at 10 William Street, Gus took me to . . .

FRED'S. Great place. It's like you're in a chic friend's very large house. Fun vibe. Delish.

SEAN'S. Formerly known as Sean's Panorama. Call it that; people will think you're a local. I don't know why they shortened it. Brad and I went here the first time we were in Sydney many years ago, and loved it. Just went back with Gus. It's right by the water on Bondi Beach. Super casual and friendly, with fantastic food. Call ahead and order the roast chicken. (I eat a lot of roast chicken, I know, but this one is amazing.) My favorite restaurant in Sydney.

ICEBERGS. Directly on Bondi Beach. An institution. Fabulous. (I like it for lunch.)

Do the HARBOUR BRIDGECLIMB SYDNEY. If I can do it, anyone can.

And DM @gussymurray and ask him to be your Aussie mate while you're in town. He's the best.

Mykonos

BELVEDERE HOTEL. This is where I was staying when I met Brad, and where we have stayed every trip since. I love it here, but I'm biased. (Also, it's in town. That's where you want to stay. Trust me.)

Favorites

TO MAEREIO. Best restaurant on the island. Tiny. No reservations. Owned by identical twin brothers. Have a glass of wine while you wait and people-watch. We go at least twice a trip. I actually want it now, just typing this. I get the omelet with potatoes. It's not on the menu, but if you ask for it, they'll make it.

KIKI'S TAVERN. For lunch. You'll have to wait. Worth it. Go to Agios Sostis Beach before or after. No music, no chairs, no crowds. Most beautiful beach on the island.

NIKO'S TAVERNA. Where I met Brad. What more is there to say?

NAUTILUS (tell Ireni I say "hi!") and KOUNELAS FISH TAVERN for fish. Both are great.

FOKOS TAVERNA. Go for lunch. You'll love it.

See a movie at the outdoor cinema, CINE MANTO!

Rent a Smartcar.

I hope you meet a Brad.

Los Angeles

I don't leave the house much in LA. But when I do . . .

CRAIG'S. It's always fun, and I love Craig and the burger. Everyone goes to Craig's.

JON & VINNY'S. We get our pizza from here every Sunday night.

VERVE COFFEE ROASTERS. When I don't go to the other place.

THE NOSH. Where I get my roast turkey breast and bagels.

SUGARFISH and SUSHI PARK. Our favorite sushi spots.

SALT & STRAW. Our favorite ice cream.

THE CHEESE STORE OF BEVERLY HILLS. My favorite place in LA. It's like you've stepped into a market in France. (When I'm in LA, I'm happy being in places that look like something other than LA.) Great cheese. Great wine. Great staff. And now they have sandwiches!

Favorites

If I go anyplace else in LA, I don't remember. Brad pretty much cooks every night. Again, he's a good egg.

Oh, and go to MALIBU SEAFOOD! But only if it's nice out. (It might be nice in town, but overcast when you get to the beach. I can't help that.)

(Also, I'm not affiliated with any of these places. I just like them. They don't even know they're in this book. And sorry for using the words "favorite," "great," and "fabulous" so much. I kept Googling synonyms for them, but it kept coming up with words I wouldn't use.)

chapter eighteen

Always . . .

Keep your passport current. (Go check when it expires now.)

Take a trip whenever you have the chance, even if you don't have someone to go with. Go alone. It'll be great, I promise. Better even.

Ask for an upgrade. (It can't hurt.)

Ask for a booth.

Say "please" and "thank you," and push your chair in when you get up from the table. (My mother taught me this early. Thanks, Mom.)

We Are Experiencing a Slight Delay

Take at least one day on every trip, and don't plan a thing. Just walk around. Get coffee. See a movie. Sleep in. Pretend you live there.

Ask the people who work at your hotel where they go to eat. Don't only go to restaurants you've read about or been told to go to, or have seen on Instagram. Mix it up, for Christ's sake.

If you don't speak the language, learn how to ask, "Do you speak English?" in whatever language they speak. And "good morning" and "good night." A tiny effort goes a long way. Also, it's just good manners. (See Mom, above.)

Pack only carry-on luggage. You don't need all that shit. (Come on, try it once. For me.)

Do at least one thing a trip that takes you out of your comfort zone. (The bridge climb counts for several trips.)

Ask your waiter their name, then introduce yourself. It makes for a nicer experience for everyone.

If you're ever rude (sometimes one gets cranky while traveling), apologize.

Always . . .

Don't blame the flight attendants when your flight is delayed.

Tip your bellman. (And if you don't have cash, tell them you're going to get some from the front desk, and then find them and tip them. When I was a bellman, often people would say, "I don't have any cash, but I'll find you later," and they never did. Once, the actress Jennifer Connelly said to me, "Hold on, I'm going to get some cash. I'll be right back." Then she left the hotel and returned a few minutes later, and gave me twenty dollars. I will always love her for that. Thank you again twenty-nine years later, Jennifer Connelly.)

Tip your concierge. (Just leave an envelope for the whole team at the end of your stay. The amount depends on how much you used the service.)

And *always* tip housekeeping. This is perhaps the most important and most overlooked. (Twenty dollars a day is a good guide.) And leave a little note thanking them for cleaning your room each day, and making it so beautiful for you to come back to. And say "good morning" and "thank you" when you pass them in the halls. And just because you're in a hotel, don't leave your room a pigsty. Remember, someone has to clean it, and they work hard.

We Are Experiencing a Slight Delay

These are things that I learned working in a hotel, and that I never forgot. I thought I'd pass them along.

And finally:

Be a gracious guest, wherever you are in the world. Don't compare it to back home. (You'll be back there soon enough.)

I'd Like to Thank

Mom and Dad, for bringing Maria and me on every single trip you ever went on. Until I was eighteen and you took a cruise to Alaska during my high school graduation. It instilled in me a love of travel that has stayed with me to this day.

My sister, Maria Abeshouse, for being my first, best travel partner. I'm sorry I wasn't more compassionate when you fell off your moped in St. Thomas when I was sixteen and you were eighteen. Even though it was your idea to rent them in the first place, I thought it was dangerous. (Also, the other passengers must have been wondering what the fuck we were doing on that cruise alone.)

My brother-in-law, Adam Abeshouse, and my nieces Emily Abeshouse and Sarah Abeshouse, for being such wonderful company on all the trips we have taken together throughout the years. And for not falling off a moped.

My mother-in-law, Debby Goreski, and her partner, John Tompkin, for being such great travel companions. I think I forgot to mention I was going to be writing about that cruise we were on. Hope it's okay. (Not that I can do anything about it now.)

My sister-in-law whom I adore, Amanda Goreski, for flying out to LA after Brad came home with me and giving me the okay.

My friend and fellow former Paramount Hotel employee, Serena Lightner, for sharing hotel and restaurant recommendations with me (not to mention many wonderful dinners) for over thirty years.

Tom McDonald for helping me curate my restaurant lists and everything else.

Jeff Richman and John Benjamin Hickey for taking me out to dinner at Craig's for my birthday. And for not singing to me. It meant the world.

My agents Jay Sures and Albert Lee at UTA for being the absolute best. (And Jay, for that dinner at Cipriani after it just opened. You know how much I wanted that reservation.)

Tony Peyrot for everything you do for me, which makes it possible for me to do stuff like write this book.

I'd Like to Thank

Kelly Ripa and Andy Cohen for your friendship and incredible support always. (There's a part of me that's still waiting for a contract role on *All My Children*, Kelly.)

Benjamin Askinas for the terrific photos you took for the front and back cover of this book. (And author photo and everything else I'm going to use them for.) I felt like Cindy Crawford.

My Aussie mate, Gus Murray. You made Australia for me, Gus. Becoming better friends during that trip was my favorite part of it. Also, the weather. Sun every day.

Mel from the Taronga Zoo, Sydney. I'm thanking you again for my private audience with the koalas, Mel. That was my favorite part of the trip. (Sorry, Gus.)

Everyone on board the *Queen Mary 2* for being so fantastic. (And Vincenza at Cunard Line for being so kind during boarding!)

Steve Hasley for always staying with our dogs, Alice and Theo, making it possible for us to travel. They love you maybe too much now.

The entire staff of the Chiltern Firehouse—Hamish, David, Rob, Rebecka, Mila, Max, Rowena, Sam, the other David,

I'd Like to Thank

Jimmy, Cleo, Michael, Katya, Oystein, James, Harrison, Haban, Grace, Sandra, Eliza, Toby, all the Matts, Bobby's Oysters, and everyone else! (If I forgot you, sorry!) For always making me feel so at home. I'll be back soon.

(Also everyone across the street at the Monocle Cafe!)

Housekeeping at every hotel I've ever stayed at (especially the Chiltern Firehouse and Mercer Hotel) for always making the room so beautiful to come back to.

At HarperCollins: Becca Putman, Rachel Elinsky, Robin Bilardello, Mary Ann Petyak, Bonni Leon-Berman, Lydia Weaver, and Diana Meunier for all your work on this book. Jackie Quaranto for being so delightful and patient.

Jonathan Burnham, my editor, for being incisive, encouraging and possessed with enough good humour (British spelling) to allow me to include him in these pages.

My oldest friend, Sal Messina, for accompanying me on that trip to Mykonos.

and

Brad for walking by my table.

About the Author

GARY JANETTI is the bestselling author of *Do you Mind if I Cancel?* and *Start Without Me.* He is a writer and producer of *Family Guy, Will & Grace, Vicious,* and *The Prince.* He lives in Los Angeles.